KT-460-011

Flyers!
The Spirit of Kitty Hawk
Ivan Rendall

Ivan Rendall was born in Birmingham in 1947 and went to school in Stourbridge, Worcestershire. He learnt to fly privately in 1965 and worked in New Zealand and Australia before joining the Royal Air Force for training as a pilot. He left the RAF and settled on the island of Anglesey as a farmer and businessman. He started writing part-time for the local press in North Wales and later worked as a television researcher for the BBC. He presented the BBC Radio 4 series 'The Spirit of Kitty Hawk' to mark the eightieth anniversary of the first flight of the Wright Brothers in 1983 and is now a freelance television producer. He continues to work for BBC Radio and Television. He is married with three children and lives in London and Worcester.

IVAN RENDALL

FLYERS!

The Spirit of Kitty Hawk
With an introduction by Frederick Forsyth

ARIEL BOOKS
BRITISH BROADCASTING CORPORATION

Published by the British Broadcasting Corporation
35 Marylebone High Street London WIM 4AA

First published 1985

© Ivan Rendall 1985

ISBN 0 563 201273 4

Typeset by Phoenix Photosetting, Chatham
Printed and bound in Great Britain by
Mackays of Chatham Ltd, Kent

This book is set in 10 on 11 point Ehrhardt

Contents

For my Mother and Father

Acknowledgements

Without the encouragement of Anne Howells, the producer of the BBC Radio 4 series 'The Spirit of Kitty Hawk', neither the programmes nor this book would have been possible. I will be forever in her debt. Sheila Ableman, of BBC Publications, has assisted me with the form and style of the book and without her help and, on occasions, her indulgence, the book would not have been finished. Frederick Forsyth generously agreed to write the Preface and I thank him warmly for his help. Of those people I have consulted in the course of my research, I thank Ivonette Wright Miller of Dayton, Ohio, for letting me talk at length about her two remarkable uncles, Royce Verdon-Roe and Cyril Tubb for telling me about A. V. Roe, Karl August von Schoenebeck for telling me about his former commander, Richthofen, and General Charles 'Chuck' Yeager who let me interrupt his busy life to tell me about it. Thanks, too, to my family: my wife Heather and children Polly, David and Katie.

I have consulted the following sources: BBC Sound Archives; BBC TV Library; the Combat Reports of James McCudden at the Public Record Office; numerous publications of the National Aeronautics and Space Administration; *The Papers of Wilbur and Orville Wright*, Vols I and II, edited by Marvin W. McFarland; *Wright Reminiscences* compiled by Ivonette Wright Miller; *The Wright Brothers, Heirs of Prometheus*, edited by Richard P. Hallion; *The Rebirth of European Aviation* by Charles H. Gibbs-Smith; *The Flying Cathedrals* by Arthur Gould Lee; *Pioneer of the Air* by G. A. Broomfield; *The World of Wings and Things* by Sir Alliott Verdon-Roe; *The Challenging Sky* by L. J. Ludovici; *Five Years in the Royal Flying Corps* by James McCudden; *McCudden VC* by Christopher Cole; *Der Rote Kampfflieger* by Manfred von Richthofen; *Lindbergh, a biography* by Leonard Mosley; *The Hero* by Kenneth S. Davis; and *The Right Stuff* by Tom Wolfe. *Across the High Frontier* by W. R. Lundgren.

Preface

When I was a boy I was intermittently possessed – like most boys –
by fads or 'crazes'.

On one occasion, having become interested for some reason in
birds (of the winged variety), I virtually memorised the entire
contents of *The Observer's Book of British Birds* and could tell a
passing chiffchaff from a siskin with no trouble at all. On another,
having chanced upon Hemingway's *Death in the Afternoon*, I
became fascinated by bullfighting. Again, with the extraordinary
absorptive power of the very young when once interested in
something, I read every book I could find about tauromachy until
the gaunt and haunted faces of Joselito and Belmonte were as
familiar as any popstar to a teenager of today.

As is customary with teenagers, these crazes were passing fads
which soon burned out, to be replaced by another and newer
interest. But one such passion did not burn out; muted it may have
become, but it has stayed the test of the passing years – a fascination for aeroplanes and the men who flew them.

I think it started with a book or film about the First World War.
Even though, as a small infant, I had dimly perceived the Spitfires
and Hurricanes of the RAF wheeling above my Kentish fields in
the Battle of Britain, it was the aces of Flanders whose exploits
first enthralled me. In boyish imagination I longed to fly with
Bishop, Ball, McCudden and Mannock against Richthofen,
Boelcke, Immelmann. Pursuing a harassed librarian to distrac-
tion I devoured everything she could find in her shelves about
these and the other aces – Guynemer, Garros, Nungesser,
Hawker.

The nearest I ever came to these heady dreams was when,
learning to fly at sixteen, I managed to overstress a sturdy and
patient Tiger Moth over the Medway while taking on, single-
handed, the entire Red Circus.

My bedroom walls were papered with pictures of Camels, Pups,
S.E.5s, Spads, Albatroses and Fokkers. Later the passion

extended to the Second World War and I worked my way steadily through every biography available – Johnnie Johnson, Douglas Bader, Bob Stanford-Tuck, George Beurling, Adolf Galland and Hans-Joachim Marseille – and created more space on the walls for Mosquitos, Spitfires, Hurricanes, Messerschmitts and Mustangs. By the time I actually got into the Air Force I had memorised all their outlines up to the MiGs, Hunters, Sabres and Javelins.

So Ivan Rendall's book has for me an especial interest, as it must have for any person intrigued to read about those extraordinary creatures – the aces. They cannot, of course, all be here; there would be too many and thus not enough space to give an illuminating pastiche of any single one.

What has been done here is to take nine careers – ten men although the Wright Brothers count as one episode – each telling the story of a man whose life formed a hinge in the history of flying. There are four pioneers, three developers of the flying art and two whose lives span the leap from air to space. What strikes one is how different – apart from the common lust to get off the ground – they all were: Blériot, clumsy, untutored and insanely brave, who crossed the Channel in a craft in which most would be daunted to cross the road; Cody the brash showman; Roe who wanted to build bigger, faster, and better. We meet McCudden, not only an ace but a sky-tactician; Richthofen, the legend; Lindbergh, victim of idolatry, tragedy and his own flaws; Yeager, the ultimate test pilot whose rocket-powered flights beyond the known frontiers opened the door to inner space; and Young, the technologist who test-flew the Phantom and went on to fly five times into space itself.

Just how different – and alike – were the first men who, without parachutes or any aids, took ramshackle string-and-wire contraptions into the clouds, and the latest, who have dared to enter the soundless, weightless sea of space, is revealed in these nine stories that span a hundred years and a million miles. Anyone who has ever looked up with yearning, or even wondered about that great vault of blue above us, will be fascinated by these stories of nine men who went there.

Frederick Forsyth
London, May 1985

1 The Wright Brothers

The golden days of autumn 1903, the sparkling sun and the petulant storms, put up a futile defence against the approach of winter. By December the whole Atlantic coast of North Carolina had succumbed: a strong north wind whistled over the dunes along Pamlico Sound and dark-tinged clouds raced each other to blot out the sun. On the morning of the 17th, the night's rain was frozen hard into the sand.

Out on the barrier beaches that morning, near the remote village of Kitty Hawk, a small group of spectators gathered round as two men tinkered with a strange-looking machine, a fragile skeleton of wood and wire covered with tightly-stretched muslin. It was an aeroplane, balanced on a rail and pointing straight into the wind.

At about ten-thirty the engine burst into life and the two propellers began to spin, urging the craft forward. One of the men climbed on to the quivering lower wing; he lay face down then let go the restraining rope; the machine leapt down the rail for several yards, then the wind gripped its wings and lifted it into the air. Like a roller coaster, it rose and dipped in an erratic flight, lasting just twelve seconds, then settled back on the ground.

The man at the controls was Orville Wright and the first to rush up and congratulate him was his brother Wilbur Wright. The cheers of the others were lost on the wind.

Between them, the Wright Brothers made four flights that day; the longest was just under a minute. Then an unkind gust of wind caught the *Flyer*, as they now called their machine, and overturned it. If they were elated by their success, or downhearted by the accident, neither emotion showed through their steady nature or ruffled their thoughtful, stoic faces; they appeared to take it all in their stride. But inside, the two brothers were bubbling; not even picking up the pieces of their smashed *Flyer* could dampen their spirits.

They knew what they had accomplished that day, and for some

time afterwards they were the only people who really did know. They had made the first ever powered, sustained and controlled flight. They had managed to fly an aeroplane under its own power, taking off and landing at the same level, and they had controlled it, albeit erratically, throughout the flight. Not even they could have foreseen what eventually followed, the tremendous speed and scale of aeronautical development, but on that day, they knew that the age of the aeroplane had dawned.

If 17 December 1903 was the birthday of the practical, powered aeroplane, then at the time, the news made little impact. Newspaper reporters did not get very excited: the flight had lasted less than a minute, the place was not even found on all maps, the only witnesses were a few local fishermen, and the pilots who claimed to have flown were two obscure brothers who did nothing to project themselves and little to project their achievement. Indeed, their actions invited press indifference and public apathy.

Later the same evening, they did send a telegram to their father at home in Ohio, telling him of their success and asking him to inform the press. He spoke to reporters, but the coverage was sparse and garbled. It is hard to blame the reporters because they had so little to go on; the Wright Brothers gave no details of the *Flyer*, nor would they release the photograph which had been taken just as it had left the ground.

The Wright Brothers' reticence is understandable. They had filed patent applications for their machine and intended to profit from it. They had paid for all their experiments themselves and saw no reason to give away their secrets, especially to other experimenters. What they failed to appreciate was that they had not just invented a device, like an egg-whisk or even the telephone; they had realised one of man's oldest and most precious dreams, to conquer the air, to fly like the birds and be free of the Earth.

Their apparent secretiveness inevitably aroused scepticism about their claim to have flown. Had they been more open, posterity might have been kinder to them, but they have gone down in history as austere, taciturn, rather puritanical men and the two stories told and retold about them are that they never flew on Sundays and they always flew in a stiff collar and tie.

That was their public image, but within the security of their family, they were outgoing and entertaining.

The Wright family was, and remains, one of those extended, happy tribes bound together by ancestry and common traditions; family occasions were times for teeming parties to reinforce the ties between the different branches and generations.

From the early 1870s, the centre of gravity for the family was a large timber house in Hawthorne Street, Dayton, Ohio, where Bishop Milton Wright and his wife Susan settled after years of peripatetic preaching. Here, the Wrights created a home and a very open and honest atmosphere for their five children, four boys and the youngest a girl: Reuchlin (b.1861), Lorin (b.1862), Wilbur (b.1867), Orville (b.1871) and Katherine (b.1874).

It was a household where the children were encouraged to experiment with ideas and taught to be resourceful. Their father was often away on business for the United Brethren Church and the children had to help their mother, who saw to it that their hands and minds were never idle. It was not a difficult task for the children were naturally inquisitive; when the bishop came home from one of his travels he brought a model helicopter made out of cork and bamboo for his six-year-old son Orville, the boys played with it and flew it, but before long, they took it to pieces to find out how it worked and then built copies and flew them.

Neither Wilbur nor Orville had a distinguished school career but at home Wilbur, especially, read voraciously in subjects that interested him. Orville read too, but he was much more inclined to experiment with problems than to read about them. While still in his teens, he built a printing press of his own design to print his own woodcuts and a little family newspaper.

Later, he and Wilbur got together to build another, larger press and together they compiled and printed a local weekly newspaper for their area, *West Side News*. Wilbur was the editor and Orville the printer. After a year, they converted it into a daily paper but they had to cease publication in the face of competition from the big local dailies. This joint boyhood venture characterised their whole lives together: unselfish cooperation in pooling their joint ideas and talents, purposeful hard work towards a common goal and a business acumen stunted by scrupulous honesty.

They were innovators rather than entrepreneurs, driven by their inventiveness and not simply by the pursuit of riches. They were thrifty and could produce a product for the market, but their honesty and openness was a drawback in business when it came to exploiting any advantage. Rather than fight a dirty circulation war, they looked elsewhere, both to make a living and to satisfy their joint intellect.

The last decade of the nineteenth century was the age of the bicycle; the ill-proportioned high-wheelers, or penny-farthings, had given way to the more practical 'safety bicycle', the design of which has remained basically unchanged to the present day.

Wilbur and Orville bought bicycles in 1892, primarily as a means of transport, but it wasn't long before they discovered that they could make a good living selling and servicing them.

Typically, they took the bicycles to pieces, rebuilt them and then, having worked out the principles of construction, built their own. It was a perfect outlet for their practical engineering skills; within four years, they had formed the Wright Cycle Company and were manufacturing and selling their own 'Wright Specials'.

The bicycle business did well and the two brothers prospered steadily but with hardly an outward ripple on their attitudes or their way of life: both remained unmarried and lived with their now widowed father and sister Katherine. Reuchlin had moved to Kansas and Lorin had married and left the parental home, but he and his young family were frequent visitors, never missing their Sunday meals at Hawthorne Street where a new generation of Wright children pounded the corridors.

Hawthorne Street was a hive of both practical and intellectual activity: 'Orv' and 'Will' would debate ferociously but without malice on a wide range of subjects from engineering to fairy stories. In the parlour, they would resort to a childish method of debate: ''tis so', ''tisn't either', ''tis', ''tisn't' . . .

It was a stimulating place for the new generation of Wright children; Grandfather Milton Wright let his grandchildren experiment with his typewriter and gaze at stereoscopic photographs of long-gone relatives. Orville and Wilbur invented a shadowgraph show: two jointed figures, a fat one called Joe Higgenbottom and a thin one called Mr Bonebrake who performed in front of a lantern; the figures were made out of sheet metal in the bicycle factory. But it was not all fun, there was the discipline from the old days too; if the little ones misbehaved, they were locked in a small room which was full of books and magazines, both as a punishment and as a means of improving their minds.

There was an intricate network of nicknames in the Wright family which ranged across the generations: Orville was 'Bubbo', Wilbur was 'Ullam', Lorin's daughter Ivonette was 'Inetz', her sister 'It' and her brother 'Toujours' or 'Whackers'. Any child who displayed bad table manners was a 'goop'.

When Ivonette's mother went shopping, she would leave the three children in the care of their uncles at the bicycle factory, where they sat amongst the whirring machinery, the spruce timber ribs, the muslin and the pungent gluepots which were the sights, sounds and smells of the Wright Brothers' latest developing passion – aeroplanes.

The air was the one element which the Victorian age failed to conquer. Steamships ploughed through the world's oceans regardless of winds and railways spanned the continents, but apart from a small band of dedicated experimenters, and a few publicity-seekers who were attracted to high public places like the Eiffel Tower to jump to their deaths in the name of science, the air was left to visionaries and science-fiction writers.

The theory that lift is generated by a wing moving through the air was not new and attempts had been made to fly in steam-powered, winged vehicles, some of which had even managed short, uncontrolled hops. Gliders, some of them rather like today's hang-gliders, were more successful but pilots had been killed in experiments and the idea of flying, except possibly in balloons, was widely held to be at best far-fetched and at worst dangerous.

Even the aeronautical buffs were divided over what form an aeroplane should take. There were those who saw aircraft in much the same way as ships: big structures floating on their wings or supported by hydrogen, powered by a steam engine and steered by a rudder. Then there were those who looked to the birds for inspiration, who wanted to ride the wind and come to terms with it. The late Charles H. Gibbs-Smith, Britain's premier air historian, labelled the two groups 'chauffeurs' and 'airmen'.

Wilbur and Orville were fascinated by the problems of flight. They read all the published material they could and sympathised with the 'airmen' more than the 'chauffeurs'. If one was going to literally 'ride the wind', then being able to control oneself in the air, like the birds, was the first requirement.

In true Wright fashion, Wilbur looked to the birds he was trying to emulate and tried to divine from them how he should tackle the problem. He went out to the prairies around Dayton and watched as buzzards maintained their balance by twisting the tips of their wings.

It was lack of any means of regaining balance which had killed a number of glider pilots; when their machines tipped a little they were unable to right them so they flipped over and crashed. What went through Wilbur's mind was: if aeroplanes could flex their wingtips like birds, they could balance like birds. If they could balance and control themselves like birds, they could fly like birds too.

From birds, the brothers moved to kites. They built a fabric biplane kite with a five-foot wingspan. It had four lines, one attached to each end of the upper and lower wings. By pulling the lines to twist the wings up on one side and down on the other, they produced the same effect as the wingtip feathers of the buzzards and could regain balance if the kite was disturbed. Equally, they could deliberately unbalance the kite, making it roll, and then reverse the pull on the lines to regain it.

When they were ready to try a man-carrying kite, they wrote to the US Weather Bureau for advice on where to find open terrain with strongish, steady winds where they could fly it. The records of the weather station at Kitty Hawk, with its strong but steady northerly autumn winds, suggested that it might be just the place. Wilbur wrote to the local postman and fisherman, Bill Tate, and from his local knowledge of the miles and miles of sand Wilbur decided to try it.

Kitty Hawk is an isolated spot on one of the barrier beaches just off the Atlantic coast of North Carolina. Although close to one of the earliest settled parts of America, the isolation of the area had once made it a favourite haunt of pirates. When the brothers arrived in September 1900, they found it was still a desolate place, an open expanse of sand dunes and a few stunted trees growing horizontally in deference to the wind. But it was perfect for flying.

The machine they experimented with that year was a hybrid; half-kite, half-glider. It was made out of spruce timber and wire and covered in muslin, with a wingspan of 17 feet; it looked rather like a set of wings from a biplane with the fuselage removed and replaced by a single elevator out in front. They started experimenting by tethering it in the wind as a gigantic kite and then operating the two controls from the ground by long lines. One set of lines was attached to the elevator, the other worked their 'wing-warping' system which twisted the trailing edge of the wingtips just like the smaller kite and the Dayton buzzards.

Gradually they learnt how to control the machine in the high winds, but not before they had a disastrous accident. After one unmanned flight, a strong gust caught hold of it as they were reeling it in and smashed it to the ground before they could right it with the controls. Many men would have given up then, but the Wright Brothers set to and repaired it with the help of a sewing-machine borrowed from Bill Tate's wife. Within a week, they had rebuilt it and were flying again.

While he was there, Orville wrote at length to his sister Katherine clearly indicating that he was enjoying a rich life at Kitty Hawk, despite the isolation. The brothers lived in a tent, and any comforts, other than eggs from the local homes, or fish, had to be ferried from the mainland. On occasions they dined with the

Tate family, especially if a wild goose had been shot, and Bill Tate became a keen assistant with the kite, trying to do his day's work in two or three hours so that he could help the Wrights.

There was plenty of warm human contact, despite the sparse population. There was free exchange of help and ideas between the 'Kitty Hawkers' and the Wrights, whose campsite was sometimes better equipped than the local homes; indeed, the brothers soon became local curiosities with their acetylene lamps and gasolene stoves. In his letters Orville told Katherine all the local gossip, observing both his hosts and his surroundings, the local storekeeper's business, the sunsets, the mockingbirds and the abundant fish. The company of these honest and lively people, their simple ways and their wild, unspoilt surroundings was clearly enriching.

He shared the seashore treasures with his nephew Milton, too, sending him a dried horseshoe crab and a bottle containing genuine seawater and sand.

Bill Tate and his brother, Dan, helped the Wrights haul the glider to some high dunes known as Kill Devil Hills to begin manned experiments. But before they could carry them out, they had to learn how to fly it; it was clearly not like a car, where one simply sat and steered; the pilot had to think and act quickly in several dimensions at once and acquiring those skills would only come with practice.

The experiments consisted of taking the glider up to the top of the highest dune which they christened 'Big Hill'. One of the brothers would lie prone on the lower wing while the other, and one of the Tates, each took a wingtip and raced down the sand with it until it reached flying speed and floated into the air. After that the pilot was on his own, gliding out over the sand gingerly trying out the two controls, the elevator to make it go up or down, and the wing warps to roll it into a turn or right it when upset by a gust. It was in the truest sense of the word 'test' flying, for they could clearly not fully understand what was going on nor what the full implications of their control movements would be: if they used the elevator to make the glider climb then the speed would fall, the wind would flow slower over the wings, lift would decline and the glider would stall. Today, pilots take all this for granted, having spent years in training, but to the Wrights it was all new and their lives depended on being able to combine their theoretical knowledge of aerodynamics with quick movement of the controls. Today, what they were doing would be far too risky even for a sport.

That year, 1900, they covered distances of up to 400 feet at speeds of up to thirty miles per hour. They went back to Dayton with a strange feeling of elation: they knew they had achieved something because they had flown, they had felt for the first time that wonderful sensation of being supported by wings rushing through the air, but they were not sure exactly where their achievement led them.

Through the winter they argued and theorised while they built another glider, No. 2, which was designed from the start to carry a pilot. It was based on the 1900 design, but it was much bigger, with a 22-foot wingspan, and it had a much more curved wing. The shape of the wing was based on calculations and lift tables worked out by a German glider pilot, Otto Lilienthal, who had been killed experimenting with methods of control in 1896. The glider was made in such a way that it could be dismantled and packed in crates for shipment to Kitty Hawk and in July 1901, the brothers were back among the sand dunes; this time they built a wooden shed right alongside Big Hill so that they could live and work close to the job.

The No. 2 glider proved to be much more of a handful than its predecessor; it was very sensitive to the controls, like a nervous thoroughbred stallion. Even small movements of the control levers had instant and sometimes alarming effects; on some early flights Wilbur had to augment the controls by shifting his weight to alter the balance of the machine and bring the nose down in order to regain flying speed. They found that by reducing the curvature of the wing, they could improve the flying characteristics, but it was still a difficult machine to fly.

When they experimented with turns, using a wing-warping system, they found that the new glider had an alarming tendency to slew round; frequently both of them were only saved by their quick wits. At the end of their second flying season, Orville and Wilbur went back to Dayton having made little progress. But they were increasingly sure of one thing: Lilienthal's calculations were wrong and if they were going to be successful, they would have to work out their own.

Back in the bicycle factory in Dayton, they started from scratch and what followed was probably the most useful series of experiments they ever carried out. To start with, their methods were crude but effective; they took a bicycle and mounted a wheel horizontally in front of the handlebars over the front wheel. The horizontal wheel was free to turn so that when they attached little winglets to the rim, and rode the bicycle forward, the wind moved over the winglets and created lift which rotated the wheel. Different shapes of winglets produced different effects on the wheel.

The next step was to build a wind tunnel. By attaching the winglets to a small balance and then placing the balance in the airflow, the lift generated by the winglet moved the balance and could be measured more accurately. Gradually, they began to build up their own tables of lift and applied them to another glider, No. 3, which began to take shape in early 1902. The wind tunnel became the basic tool of the aerodynamicist and has been in use ever since.

In deciding to ignore Lilienthal's tables and use their own figures they were taking a bold course for two relatively new experimenters; not only were they risking their necks if they were wrong, they were also inviting the ridicule of the aeronautical world for challenging what had been an accepted basis for lift calculations. But they stuck to their own theories.

At this stage in their careers, they were still quite open in the way they discussed their scientific findings and in September 1901 Wilbur delivered a 10,000-word discourse on their experiments to the Western Society of Engineers. They had set out with the intention of making some contribution to aeronautical knowledge, but they did not yet see aeronautics as a business which might take over from their bicycles even though they did take on staff to allow them to continue with their experiments.

Being bicycle engineers and riders helped them in many ways: their skills in lightweight engineering were vital in making the very light but very strong structures, and by riding bikes they were familiar with the art of balancing on an unstable, moving machine by leaning over when going round corners.

The No. 3 glider showed the results of their winter of experimental work. Basically, it looked much the same as their previous machines, but closer examination revealed that the wings were much longer, at over thirty-two feet, and they were narrower and much thinner. The elevator was still out in front, but they had added a fixed vertical fin at the rear. The wing warps were now operated by a cradle which the pilot lay in and moved with his hips. Back at Kitty Hawk in the autumn of 1902, the performance of the new glider was not much of an improvement on their exploits of the previous year at first; it still had a tendency to slew round in a turn.

The brothers always took it in turns to fly; one day, when Orville was flying he noticed that one wing was slightly higher than the other and so operated the cradle to level the wings. But instead of levelling them, the higher wing went even higher and the glider began to slide towards the lower wing from about thirty feet. Orville struggled with the controls, using them violently to their fullest extent but to no avail, the glider slid sideways and backwards and crashed. Fortunately Orville escaped without a scratch.

At first, they thought that the reason must be lack of practice but eventually, they realised that there was still a basic problem with the design of the controls. They wrestled with the problem by practical experiment during the day and with mental activity at night. It was Orville who eventually came up with the answer: when the wing warp was operated, it increased the drag on the warped wing, causing the slewing effect; in addition, the fixed tailplane was aiding the process by offering resistance to the airflow when the wing warps turned the whole machine. By making the tailplane moveable, and linking it to the wing-warping cradle, it could be turned to compensate for the warp drag and it also offered no resistance.

The changes were a dramatic success and for the next few weeks, hardly a day went by (except Sundays which they kept as the Sabbath) without both of them skimming over the dunes, turning and banking just like the buzzards. By the end of that season, they had become proficient pilots and knew they had solved the basic problems of control. The three control devices, though operated differently, have remained unchanged in principle to the present day: the elevator, the rudder and the ailerons (wing warps). Learning to use them in conjunction with each other, to make a coordinated turn, is what every pilot learns in his first flying lessons.

For the Wright Brothers, the end of their experimental season in 1902 was the culmination of three years of thinking and theorising, months of hard practical work, weeks of dangerous experiment and nights spent tossing and turning in their bunks at the Kitty Hawk campsite, mentally grappling with aeronautical problems while Atlantic gales lashed their shed. Only with their joint single-mindedness of purpose and rigorously honest and truthful pursuit of knowledge could they have achieved what they did. Their upbringing in the hands of a clergyman had instilled in them from an early age that truth was indivisible. It is ironic that their search for a scientific truth was helped by a fundamental belief in truth which arose out of a religious faith. It was now only a matter of time, and a little more hard work, before they could achieve their real goal of powered flight. Their breakthrough lay not so much in the length of the flights they had made (the longest was 622 feet, lasting 26 seconds), but in the knowledge that they had gained about control, and in their new lift calculations.

Inevitably, news that they were working along very productive lines had leaked out from their own contacts, from Wilbur's lecture and through the several experiments who had come to Kitty Hawk to observe them. The main competition in America came from the Secretary of the Smithsonian Institution, Professor Samuel Langley; he had devoted nearly twenty years to the problem of powered flight but by 1903 had only a few model flights to show for his efforts.

Langley, who had huge resources behind him, tried to contact the Wrights through their friend and mentor, the now elderly engineer and aeronautical experimenter, Octave Chanute. He explained that what he was most interested in was their methods of control. He was building a monstrous machine called the *Aerodrome* and though he expected to be able to profit from the work done by the Wrights, he kept his own machine very secret. The Wrights firmly but politely refused to let him in on their methods. But it made them think: if they were that far ahead of Langley, they might be able to take their work even further once they had a practical powered aeroplane. Consequently, they became less prepared to divulge the details of their experiments.

Back in Dayton they began adapting their glider design for powered flight. There were two new problems to overcome: building an engine which was powerful enough to drive it while being light enough to be carried by it, and making propellers to turn that power into forward motion. No engineering company could produce an engine to their specification so they designed and built one themselves with the help of a local engineer in Dayton, Charlie Taylor. It was a simple design, 'knocked up' from sketches and discussions; but it worked. They found that little was really known about how propellers worked on ships – shipwrights used trial and error to produce the right shape for a particular vessel – so they started from scratch and went back to their own scientific way of doing things. They discovered that a propeller was really just a wing which generated lift by being rotated through the air, just like the model helicopter all those years ago. By applying their own lift calculations, they worked out the best shape.

By late September 1903 they were on their way back to Kitty Hawk with their powered machine. The basic design was similar to the last glider except for the engine and the two propellers, but the wings had now spread to over forty feet. The propellers were driven by bicycle chains, rotating them in opposite directions so that the torque would not pull the machine to one side. When they reached the campsite, their first job was to rebuild the shed which was almost in ruins after the storms of the previous winter, but they soon had it habitable again and as snug as possible. They built a second shed to house the powered machine and while they waited for it to arrive from Dayton in its crates, they brushed up their flying skills in the 1902 glider. That autumn, they were under a certain amount of pressure: Professor Langley was about to attempt a flight with his *Aerodrome* and on 8 October his trial went ahead in Washington. The huge, tandem-winged monster was catapulted off the top of a houseboat to hang momentarily in the air before splashing into the Potomac. It was an embarrassing failure for Langley.

It was not in the Wrights' character to gloat at Langley's débâcle, but when it was rumoured that he was going to try again as soon as his machine was repaired, they redoubled their efforts. A succession of small but frustrating problems with the engine and the propellers held them up at first: the engine ran roughly and threatened to shake the whole structure to bits, then the propeller shafts broke under the strain and had to be sent back to Dayton, to Charlie Taylor, for repair.

When they got the sprockets back, these worked loose on the propellers. Once again, bicycle technology helped: they used tyre cement to make the joint and it held for a while but then the shafts developed cracks and this time Orville went back to Dayton to make new ones with better steel.

On 8 December, Langley was ready again, and the press and officials gathered to watch. The launch was a dismal failure; the *Aerodrome* buckled amidships seconds after the launch and dropped straight into the river, nearly drowning the pilot. That week, the idea of manned flight became a joke in the press. One paper suggested that Professor Langley should turn to submarine research and this flippant attitude summed up public opinion, reinforcing the belief that manned flight was impossible. At cocktail parties and church socials, armchair theorists could smugly lay down the law that if God had intended man to fly, he would have given him wings.

Orville and Wilbur were blissfully unaware of the drubbing their hapless competitor was getting at the hands of the press and the society wags. At Kitty Hawk life went on as usual. At the end of the week, the powered machine was ready for flying again but the brothers spent Sunday, 13 December, serenely among the dunes, reading, resting and free from work.

On the Monday morning they tossed a coin to see which brother would make the first attempt and Wilbur won. He managed to get airborne, but he climbed far too steeply and after about three seconds, came down with a bump. On the 17th they were ready again and it was Orville's turn: he started off well, but as the speed increased he found that control of the elevator in the front was quite difficult; it was balanced too near the centre and consequently it turned itself too far in one direction, and then, when Orville corrected it, it went too far in the other direction. As a result, the aircraft rose to about ten feet and then dipped back towards the ground again. Erratic the flight certainly was, and it ended abruptly when Orville failed to catch a dip in time – but he had done it.

Their friends at Kitty Hawk, the Tates and their neighbours who had helped the Wrights over the years, did not see the flight as all that amazing; after all, they had seen both brothers glide much further the previous year. But for Orville and Wilbur, it was the end of one era and the beginning of a new one. They would no longer make the annual pilgrimage to Kitty Hawk to suffer the mosquitoes and the privations, nor enjoy the simple surroundings and the friendly people; they knew that they had mastered what had eluded Langley and all the others and that if they were careful and businesslike they could profit from their work.

For five years their achievement was hardly noticed; they did not try to keep it a secret, but they gave away few details for fear that they would be copied and their patent applications therefore compromised. They did invite the press to watch them fly near Dayton in the summer of 1904, but it was only a small hop and the reporters went away with their disbelief merely hardened. The brothers did little to encourage them back, for the reports which they saw of their activities were so inaccurate that they built a wall of silence against the press.

The first published eyewitness account of the Wright Brothers' flying did not appear in a learned journal or a racy newspaper but in perhaps the most obscure and esoteric publication of the time – *Gleanings in Bee Culture*. The Editor, Amos I. Root, came to Dayton, unannounced, in 1905 and saw a later model of the *Flyer* flying at the brothers' new test area at Huffman prairie. He wrote a vivid account of what he saw, likening the *Flyer* to a great white locomotive in the air, and to him goes the honour of being the first ever aviation correspondent!

From behind their wall of semi-silence, the Wright Brothers were busy trying to profit from their work. The British, French and American Governments showed some interest but what they really wanted was not so much to buy an aeroplane, as an insight into the Wrights' methods. The Wrights were aware of this and tried to negotiate a deal which allowed them to demonstrate the *Flyer* after signing a contract which included a money-back guarantee if they failed to meet the government's specification. It was not the way governments liked to do business. At one point the brothers came close to a deal with the French Government for a million francs but when it was suggested that the contract be increased to one and a quarter million, the additional sum being distributed amongst certain unnamed officials who had the power to make the deal go through, Wilbur would have none of it and preferred to abandon the negotiations rather than submit to dishonesty.

By 1908 they had made some money out of their *Flyers* but not much, and over those five years their secrets had gradually leaked out. In France other aircraft were flying; most were of bizarre design by comparison with the *Flyers*, but they flew in public. The Wright Brothers realised that the time had come for them to make a public demonstration. They also believed that the first application of the aeroplane would be for military reconnaissance and so Orville stayed in America to demonstrate the *Flyer* to the US Army while Wilbur went to Paris where he gave a breathtaking display and confounded the disbelievers. He took passengers and flew before thousands of excited Parisians. It was a truly thrilling spectacle, but it was too late to sell many aeroplanes; the Wright Brothers' secrets were out and governments knew that it was only a matter of time before there would be other aircraft to choose from.

Harry Harper, one of the first air correspondents in Europe, went to Paris and found the great pioneer living much as he had done at Kitty Hawk. Wilbur had a bed in the shed where he worked and he refused all local hospitality; he was as taciturn as ever despite the clear message from the Paris displays that publicity, though possibly distasteful, would help to sell aeroplanes. Anxious as he may have been to sell his wares, he remained true to himself; when Harper asked him why he said so little, Wilbur observed that the bird who did most talking was the one which did the least flying – the parrot!

In America, Orville delayed going to Washington to display the *Flyer* for the Army because his nephew, Milton Wright, was seriously ill and, once again, other matters were judged more important than business. When he did go, he met with disaster; a spar broke while flying an army officer on a demonstration flight and the weakened structure broke up in mid-air and crashed to the ground. The army officer was killed, the first aerial passenger to die; Orville was very seriously injured.

While Orville was in hospital he and Wilbur exchanged a fretful correspondence; they had a close relationship even for brothers and their very closeness was the source of much of their inspiration and their success. They did not like working apart – everything they did, they tried to do together – but that year they had to do without one another. Wilbur had been offered a prize if he would fly across the English Channel but Orville begged him not to try it unless they were together, and so it never happened.

After the triumph of the 1908 display in Paris the Wright Brothers were given a rather belated reception in their home town of Dayton. The bands were out, medals were struck and banners strung across the street. But recognition did not stop other pilots from copying their ideas: one man was a particular thorn in their side – Glenn Curtiss, an ex-motorcycle racing rider who, they felt, had clearly infringed their patents. The brothers became involved in long and often bitter patent suits and Wilbur especially spent a lot of time in the courts.

Wilbur died in 1912 of typhoid fever, and with his death, much of the magic of the Wright Brothers ended: Orville was the inventor, he was always bubbling over with ideas, but Wilbur had been the one to carry them through. It was Wilbur who would stop Orville from inventing and push them into practical experiments.

Orville continued the patent suits, but the steam had gone out of the fight and after Wilbur's death a new fight developed: the Smithsonian Institution denied that the Wrights were the first powered aviators and so, in 1928, Orville rebuilt the original *Flyer* and sent it to the Science Museum in London.

He did it because to deny that the original *Flyer* was the first practical aeroplane was, to him, a great untruth and he could not abide untruths. It was also a great injustice both to him and his dead brother. As long as the Smithsonian denied them their place in history and the *Flyer* its place in science, and while they dallied with other claims, the aircraft would remain in exile amongst people who, Orville felt, appreciated its true significance, even though it hurt him bitterly to keep the aircraft outside America. That was the stuff of which Orville Wright was made.

In 1943, the Smithsonian recanted, and when war dangers no

longer prevented its shipment, the *Flyer* came back to America. Orville did not live to see it; he died in 1948. Millions of dollars were offered to build a special museum for it; possibly it should have gone to wonderful, windswept Kitty Hawk, but Orville's executors sold the *Flyer* to the US Government for $1 and it occupies a central position in the main exhibition at the National Air and Space Museum in Washington owned, appropriately, by the Smithsonian Institution. Around it are grouped the other principal historic American aircraft: Lindbergh's *Spirit of St Louis*, Chuck Yeager's *Glamorous Glennis*, the X-1 – the first aircraft to fly faster than sound – the X-15, and a host of space capsules. High above it is a small model of the Langley *Aerodrome*.

Today, the date of the Wright Brothers' first powered flight at Kitty Hawk is almost universally regarded as the birthday of the practical, powered aeroplane. Today, too, the two country brothers, with their impeccable, all-American credentials, have a firmly-rooted place in both the history and mythology of America: national heroes and fathers of powered flight and pioneer pilots in the world's most successful aeronautical country.

In Wilbur's life it was never so; in Orville's, only in the very last years. If the Wright Brothers had been outgoing, gregarious people, willing to project themselves and their achievement, they might have not only made their fortune but spared themselves the lifelong battles for reward and recognition. After all, it would have made an excellent newspaper story even then; two God-fearing country boys, original inventors who had stood on their own two feet, pitted against an élitist aeronautical Establishment caught in an act of its own aeronautical folly. What shapes history is often not so much what people actually do, but how it is received and recorded at the time, and much of that depends on the people concerned. Largely because of their personalities, the Wright Brothers had an extremely bad press. They were stubborn and they did things their own way; indeed, persistence with their own ideas was one of the main ingredients of their success in the air. They had used their own money for their experiments, had worked very hard and placed themselves in physical danger, and they saw no reason to share the secrets of their success with other people – especially other pilots – at least until they had been rewarded for their efforts. The essence of their success was a rare combination of qualities coming together at just the right time: scientific inquisitiveness, practical imagination and engineering skill powered by an invisible current of single-mindedness of purpose and intellectual and physical courage.

In many ways, the Wright Brothers embody the dichotomy of their age; the work ethic, uprightness and self-respect versus the superficial world of the press and high society; the struggle between science and ingenuity on the one hand and Faith and the Word of God on the other. Unfettered freedom of thought occasionally clashed with unshakeable belief in The Right; absolute honesty never faltered in the face of the realities of business.

They were religious men and their righteous attitude, never flying on Sundays, their simple honesty and their obvious distaste for publicity made them outsiders, even freaks, in what was a shallow, champagne age. They shrouded their achievements from the public and they did it primarily in pursuit of profit. It's hardly surprising that the press and the public never warmed to them. But, just the same, they were very great men.

2 Louis Blériot

Wilbur's display in Paris may have thrilled the crowds but ever since 1903, there had been a campaign in France to discount the Wright Brothers, to deny what they said they had done and to establish French claims to have conquered the air. (There are still Frenchmen, and others, who argue that the Wrights' position as the first real powered aviators is bogus.)

It was pique more than anything else: ever since the Montgolfier Brothers' balloon had drifted over Paris in 1783, Frenchmen had regarded their country as the true home of aviation and their response to the Wrights' claims was a bout of knee-jerk nationalism.

At least in France there was enthusiasm for aviation, even if it was sometimes expressed rather nationalistically, and Paris was undoubtedly the centre of European aviation. In Britain, dozing behind its sea defences and complacent in its imperial grip on much of the world, there was at best an aloof indifference and not a little sublime ignorance. In 1906, a quote in the *Daily Mail* said it all: 'Great Britain and the British Empire stand easily in the van of progress. We know more about the science of aeronautics than any other country in the world. As yet we have not attempted to apply our knowledge, but silently and quietly we have been studying the subject, exhausting every possible theory and fact until today our scientists may lay claim to have conquered the air on paper. To achieve the victory in practice will not be a difficult matter.'

Three years later, one flight changed all that.

The villagers of Les Baraques slept fitfully on the night of 24–5 July 1909; it was a calm night and the sound of a car driving along the coast road from Calais could be heard for miles. The car pulled up near a disused barn just outside the village; two men got out and scanned the sky for a sign that the wind might get up again; but calmness prevailed, and they sensed a good morning for flying.

One of the men was on crutches and limping badly. He was a large man with a prominent nose, dark-rimmed but alert eyes and a walrus moustache; he spoke to his companion in short bursts of inelegant but authoritative French, expresssing his irritation at the crowd of spectators around the barn. His name was Louis Blériot.

It was 3.30 on a Sunday morning, but all around the barn there was a bustle of activity: in the yard stood a small aircraft, a monoplane; mechanics swarmed around it, working by the light of acetylene lamps. They started the engine several times to warm it up; on one occasion, a dog barked at the machine and charged the propeller and was killed.

As soon as Blériot arrived, he took charge of the preparations. When the sun came up over the roofs of the cottages, he ordered the aircraft pushed out into the field. He mounted it and eased himself painfully into the cockpit (his legs had been burnt badly by an exhaust on an earlier flight); his crutches were strapped to the side. Then the engine was started again and the mechanics all rushed to the rear to hang on to the tail; Blériot opened the throttle wide; the engine bellowed healthily, covering him and his helpers in a thin film of oil from the exhaust ports. On a signal from his companion, the men let go of the tail and the little aeroplane sped across the grass and bounced into the air.

In the cockpit Blériot kept the throttle wide open; he climbed steeply to clear the telegraph wires at the far end of the field and they passed just beneath the wheels. Ahead the clifftops loomed, speckled with people, heads upturned, watching him go, then suddenly the coast dropped away beneath to the flat-calm waters of the Channel. Once over the water, he levelled out and eased back the power from the little engine and headed out to sea. Spectators watched him disappear into the haze, then strained their ears as the note of his engine gradually faded. Out in the Channel, a French destroyer, the *Escopette*, was standing by as his escort; when she saw him go, she billowed smoke and followed.

At 45 mph and just two hundred and fifty feet above the sea, Blériot was soon quite alone over the grey waters of the Channel with neither the French nor the British coast in sight. He had no compass and the wind was getting up, blowing him to the north. After twenty lonely minutes a sharp horizon began to emerge out of the mist; it gradually turned into the green of the English countryside. Blériot aimed for a gap in the cliffs and was soon once again over dry land. As he approached a landing ground, the wind got up and was quite fierce; the gusts buffeted his light machine; just as he was about to touch down, the wind caught him and tipped him nose-up; the propeller snapped as it touched the ground and he skidded to an undignified halt.

However bad the landing, Louis Blériot was overjoyed for he had succeeded, he was the first pilot to cross the Channel. Before long, he was surrounded by soldiers, policemen and well-wishers, including Frenchmen eager to welcome their countryman; he became an instant hero. Two days later an Englishman, Hubert Latham, set out on the same quest but failed, crashing into the sea. Even if he had made it, history hardly ever has a place for those who come second and so it was Blériot who went into the history books.

Famous though Louis Blériot certainly became, he was, by most accounts, a terrible pilot: he was uncoordinated, impatient and erratic. By 1909, when he made the Channel flight, he had experimented with a whole variety of ideas and though his contribution to the popularisation of aviation was enormous, his scientific contribution was marginal. Where the Wright Brothers had experimented logically and scientifically, Blériot attacked the problems of flight impulsively and quixotically. In many ways, he was typical of the European approach. There is no doubting his physical courage; like Orville and Wilbur he was fearless when it came to trying out his machines, but in his case, especially with some of the more bizarre examples, he risked even greater dangers.

And he was different from the Wrights in another respect too; he loved the publicity. After the Channel flight, his aircraft was put on display in Selfridges, he was driven through the streets of London and Paris to wild applause in an open car. He was fêted throughout Europe as one of the pioneers of aviation. He pocketed the £1000 prize offered for a Channel-crossing by Lord Northcliffe and orders for Blériot aircraft came in from all over the world; Louis prospered in fame and fortune. His contribution to aviation was different from the Wrights, but nevertheless it was a great one; in a single flight of thirty-seven minutes he woke up Britain and showed the world that aircraft were no longer mere lethal toys, they were a serious means of transport and they were here to stay.

Louis Blériot had graduated from engineering school at the turn of the century, just the right moment for an ambitious and technically-minded young man; the motorcar was all the rage, the status symbol and the plaything of the rich, and France took to it with zest. The automobile created a big new market for accessories and with his quick and inventive mind, Blériot made a fortune selling articles such as footwarmers, licence plates and acetylene headlamps to motorists. As fast as he made his fortune in the motor trade, he spent it on another French obsession of the time – aviation.

The sketchy reports from America that the Wright Brothers had made a powered flight in 1903 galvanised the French aeronautical Establishment into an effort to hold off the challenge. While there was no public evidence of Orville and Wilbur's achievements, there was still room for France to conquer the air and do it publicly. In 1904, a rich French aerophile, Henry Deutsch de la Meurthe, and an expatriate Irish lawyer, Ernest Archdeacon, banded together under the auspices of the Aéro-Club to offer a prize of 50,000 francs for the first flight over a measured kilometre. Archdeacon also offered a silver cup worth 2000 francs for a flight of 25 metres and 1500 francs for a flight of 100 metres.

The prizes were designed to stimulate European aviation, and in one way they were admirable: Paris became the centre for European aviation; the parks and the open spaces around the city, the Bagatelle, the Bois de Boulogne and Issy became occasional experimental airfields and fashionable citizens made excursions to see the aviators try out their latest inventions. But the prizes had another effect, especially on men like Blériot who was impatient to fly. For him it was a case of getting into the air as quickly as possible, for the prizes, for the personal achievement, and for the glory of France.

In 1905, Blériot commissioned a float-glider from Gabriel Voisin, a man who specialised in building machines to the specifications of customers. He had made a glider for Archdeacon and the one he made for Blériot was very similar. Voisin offered to test-fly it; it was towed behind a motorboat and rose into the air where it was uncontrollable and crashed into the water, nearly drowning Voisin.

In 1906, Blériot was back with a powered aircraft, the Blériot III, a seaplane based on his own ideas. On little more than a whim, he had decided that wings should be elliptical; even with a powerful 24-hp Antoinette engine, it never rose into the air.

The next Blériot machine was a modified hotchpotch of his Model III, incorporating a host of ideas from other sources. He and Voisin jointly worked on the modifications and the result showed as much about their characters as it did about their ideas. Blériot bull-headedly persisted with his ellipsoidal concept which was the basis of the tailplane; Voisin designed the main wings and front elevator along the Wright Brothers' lines and this time, it had two ailerons inspired by a Frenchman, Esnault-Pelterie, who had originally got the idea from the Wrights and then abandoned it. It was still a seaplane, powered now by two engines driving pusher propellers. It never flew, so Blériot and Voisin modified it again. This time they turned it into a land plane and renamed it the Blériot IV. It had an even more powerful 50-hp Antoinette engine, and on 12 November 1906, they took it to the Bagatelle to test it. Fortunately for both of them, it broke up on the ground.

Later that day, Blériot and Voisin witnessed one of the most successful flights in Europe up to that time; a rather shaky milestone in the persistence of aviators, if not the scientific advancement of aviation, was passed. Alberto Santos-Dumont was at the Bagatelle that afternoon with a very strange-looking machine: it had box-kite wings right at the back, with just a propeller behind; the pilot stood between the wings and in front of him stretched a long neck which finished in a combined rudder and elevator. Its shape was rather like a duck in flight and this design (elevator first) became known as the 'canard'. It had no ailerons or wing warps but Santos-Dumont managed to fly 220 metres, more than double the distance needed to claim the Aéro-Club prize. The crowd at the Bagatelle cheered heartily as Santos-Dumont landed and he was acclaimed as the hero of European aviation.

Before long, Blériot broke with Voisin and when his next machine, the Blériot V, made its appearance in 1907, its form owed much to Santos-Dumont except that it was a monoplane and not a biplane. It made a few hops, but it never flew.

Later the same year, the Blériot VI appeared. It was named *Libellule*, or dragonfly, and as the name implied, it had tandem wings which owed a lot to the design of the ill-fated Langley *Aerodrome* of 1903. It too managed some hops but no real flight and though it had moveable surfaces at the wingtips, Blériot still failed to understand the full implications of control; they were there to stabilise the aircraft if it was disturbed, not to bank it deliberately into a turn as the Wrights had done. In November he brought out his third design that year, the Blériot VII, which owed most of its design to him; it was a monoplane which was a sign of the direction Blériot was heading in but it was unsuccessful.

In 1908, he improved on it with the Blériot VIII. This time it had huge flap ailerons and, though ungainly and unmanoeuvrable, he made about thirty take-offs and a flight of some seven hundred metres. Blériot had managed to get into the air at last but he was behind the field in France.

In January 1908, the Deutsch-Archdeacon prize of 50,000 francs was won at Issy by Henry Farman, an Englishman who lived in France, flying an aeroplane built by Blériot's old friend Gabriel Voisin. The design had many similarities with the Wright *Flyers*, but it still had no ailerons and Farman had to make all the turns with rudder alone, a feat of flying skill by any yardstick but, with the benefit of hindsight, more a demonstration of how far behind the Wrights the Europeans were.

Farman issued a challenge to the Wrights: a race for a cash prize. Such gestures were not in the Wright character to accept, but the brothers began to see that the time had come to demonstrate in Europe if there was to be any hope of selling their *Flyers* before the Europeans managed to emulated them. Wilbur's display was stunning and only the most die-hard detractors would not admit his mastery of design and control. Blériot saw him fly and was clearly impressed and, though guarded in his comment, he had to admit that it was a marvellous display of skill.

Blériot struggled with his aerodynamics but the next two models, the IX and the X, were unmemorable. No doubt influenced by the Wrights, the X reverted to a biplane design. Then he got together with Raymond Saulnier and together they built the Blériot XI, a monoplane, but this time with a full wing-warping system: the trailing edges of the wingtips were flexible and could be moved up and down by using the control column, giving real control of roll. It was the Blériot XI which crossed the Channel in July 1909, setting Europe alight with wonderment.

Orders for Blériots came from far and wide and Blériot himself toured Europe making public appearances and courting potential customers. Customers were glad to be seen in his company: the Prince of Rumania and his wife rode with him round Bucharest and the crowd surged around them, lifting the car and carrying it bodily around the racecourse.

1909 was a golden year for European aviation: Wilbur's display the previous year had spurred pilots into action and many of them had bought Wright machines. The high point of the year was a show at Rheims just a month after Blériot's crossing of the Channel; he was the star attraction. It was at one and the same time a high-society binge and a gladiatorial contest: pilots raced at ground-level, for cash prizes, before the eyes of the rich who looked on from covered grandstands eating sumptuous meals while getting their vicarious thrills. The local champagne houses put up 200,000 francs in prize money, enough to ensure that experienced pilots like Blériot and Farman competed as well as the crop of newly-fledged novices. The most coveted prize was the International Aviation Cup, otherwise known as the Gordon Bennett Trophy after the American publisher who had presented it. It was awarded, together with 25,000 francs, for the highest absolute speed attained at the show. Louis Blériot, with a re-engined aircraft, was hot favourite.

One of the fiercest competitors was from the United States, a tough man with whom the Wrights had tangled over patents, the ex-motorcycle racer Glenn Curtiss. The Great Show at Rheims shot him to instant stardom too, for he won the Gordon Bennett Trophy for America in a hard-fought race with Blériot whom he beat by just six seconds.

But Blériot prospered from his aircraft which were sold all over the world and many were still in use five years later when the Great War started and they served in that war. Louis Blériot's contribution to the pioneering era of aviation is a great one; he was fortunate in the timing of his Channel crossing but he did precisely what the Wrights' had failed to do – he helped to popularise the aircraft and really show its potential. He wasn't a scientist, he was a doer and damn the consequences; his contribution to aviation was not scientific, it was in sheer boldness.

3 Samuel Franklin Cody

Farnborough Common used to be a rugged Hamshire beauty spot, a rough hillocky landscape of copses and spinneys around rolling, open clearings of tufted grass. Sometimes, the Army came up from Aldershot to camp in the clearings and soldiers joined the local visitors, the picnickers and walkers, the courting couples and the young tearaways on their newfangled bicycles. But when the War Office built its Balloon Factory there in 1899, just off the London road behind the Swan Inn, the local landmarks gradually began to disappear: Jersey Brow, Watts Common, Ball Hill and Laffan's Plain, all succumbed to the relentless advance of the hangars, workshops and runways of the Royal Aircraft Establishment at Farnborough, a name synonymous with experimental aviation.

At a spot now covered by the RAF Officers' Mess, on 16 October 1908, the first powered flight in Britain was made by British Army Aeroplane No. 1. Its design, though much bigger than a Wright *Flyer* and as yet without wing-warping, owed a lot to the Wright Brothers' ideas. But its elegant lines, its robustness and much more besides, were the original work of its pilot that day, the man who designed it and built it, the most colourful of all aviation pioneers – Samuel Franklin Cody.

The common was rough ground for aircraft, the long grass hid bumps, rabbit-holes and rotting tree-stumps, but just south of the Balloon Factory, up a small incline, there was a flattish area known as Swan Inn Plateau. On that October day, spectators watched from all the best vantage points: Cody taxied the big biplane towards the plateau; the powerful Antoinette engine pulled it up the slope with ease; from his seat behind the engine, he could see a line of trees in the distance but he judged he could fly and land before he hit them; there was a little copse much nearer, but he lined up the nose just to the left to avoid it.

He made a final check of the aircraft and the controls, then he opened the throttle: the aircraft surged forward, wallowing at first over the uneven ground, then, after a short run, the rushing autumn air gripped the wings, lifted the weight off the wheels and it leapt into the air.

It climbed quickly to about thirty feet then Cody levelled off; he could not see ahead very well so after a few seconds, remembering the trees, he eased off the power and moved the control column forwards to bring the nose down to land; the aircraft responded, but as he peered forward, to his horror, he saw that the copse was now dead ahead, the wind had blown him off course and he could not possibly land before hitting the trees.

He opened the throttle again and banked over to the left and just cleared them with one wing. He struggled with the controls to level the wings again, then he felt an ominous and heavy shudder through the whole structure of the aircraft as the left wingtip hit the ground; there was a wheel on the wingtip which protected it from too much damage and, miraculously, he did manage to right the wings. But all the manoeuvring had changed his course yet again and brought him closer to the ground. Now he was heading straight for another copse, once again well below a safe level. He banked left again, passing between two clumps of trees, but now he was too close to the ground and when the wingtip wheel hit the ground again the aeroplane slewed round in a crumpled heap.

A rather battered but unhurt Cody emerged jubilant from the wreckage; he had flown a very respectable quarter of a mile but had finished up with a broken aeroplane.

Coming just a few months after Wilbur Wright's impeccable flying display in France, Cody's achievement seemed to many people to be nothing remarkable, but it was the first powered flight in Britain and at the time Britain was very backward in aeronautical thinking. Cody had a long way to go, especially in roll control; he was only then at the point where the Wrights had been five years earlier, but his flight was the culmination of a series of trials of which he was the architect.

If the flight itself was not all that remarkable, then the man himself was. Samuel F. Cody was a big man in every sense: he weighed sixteen stone, he was immensely strong, he wore his hair down to his shoulders under a large sombrero hat, had a goatee beard and immaculately waxed moustaches; he was warm-hearted, instantly friendly and courteous and his mind held a vast store of knowledge and experience on a wide range of subjects. He was illiterate; he could barely write his own name and up to the time of the flight, though he was officially the British Army's Chief Kiting Instructor, he was more widely known as a music-hall artiste specialising in Wild West shows distinguished by his own demonstrations of sharpshooting and skill with a lasso.

He was no fake as a cowboy, he was the genuine thing: he had driven cattle across America and fought Red Indians. The first man to make a powered flight in Britain was a very American citizen.

Samuel Franklin Cody was born in 1861 into a frightening, shadowy world, which in barely two decades gave rise to the most powerful legend in history – the unpredictable anarchy, the violent and physically-demanding reality of the American Wild West.

When his father came home after four years' fighting for the Confederacy in the American Civil War, the infrastructure of the once prosperous community around Birdville, Texas, had been shattered: the family farm and vineyard was run down, neighbours had upped and left, there were no slaves to do the labouring and a wave of lawlessness prevailed. The Cody family moved north, filed a claim, built a house on an isolated spot and made a living the Texan way: they rounded up and branded wild cattle from the plains; teams of tough men then drove them hundreds of miles to the railheads and shipped them to the hungry towns in the industrial northern states. Young Samuel Cody's life was dominated by acquiring the skills to join that lifestyle: he lived in the saddle; he became an expert with a lasso and a whole range of firearms and at the age of twelve, he joined the cowboys and went on his first long cattle drive.

In 1874 he came home to see his parents. While he was there the ranch was attacked at night by Red Indians; Cody was shot in the leg but he managed to drag himself away; in the distance, he saw the house and buildings burning. He managed to reach the next ranch and was taken to hospital in Fort Worth. The cavalry were despatched to his home, but they found only ashes, no sign of his parents, brothers or sister. Still only thirteen, he went back to being a cowboy.

For the next seven years he lived a rigorous life on the plains and in the cattle towns of Texas. He learned his job from the bottom up and he was never content simply to be good at what he did, he became an expert. He mastered the tools of a cowboy's trade: the lasso, the whip, the bowie knife, the pistol, the rifle and, above all, the horse; weaving in and out of lumbering longhorn cattle and rounding up strays, he developed a supreme sense of balance and physical dexterity.

Life on the cattle drives was tough and as Cody grew in size, so he grew in strength too, and in his late teens he had a densely muscled body. But he did not just grow in physical stature; he developed a strong and remarkably rounded character too. His life was frequently violent, vulgar and dominated by the cult of the cowboys he lived with, but he had an inner strength and individual spirit which meant he was never submerged in the lifestyle. He was highly intelligent and learnt quickly from every experience and at twenty, he had matured into a fearless, self-reliant and purposeful adult.

He was restless too; though a master of his trade as a cowboy, he was always looking for new horizons. He hunted buffalo for a time, shooting them from horseback at full gallop; he broke in horses for the biggest horse-market in the world in San Antonio. (On a chance visit to Fort Worth, he found his parents and sister Mandy who had escaped from the Indian attack, too, though all his brothers had been killed.) In 1881, at the age of twenty, he was made a trail boss, in control of a team of heavy-drinking, wild cowboys, and he crowned his cowboy career with a great feat of cattle-driving: he drove 3000 head of cattle from Texas to Montana, nearly 1400 miles, in 103 days, and when he delivered the valuable herd virtually intact, the new owner was so pleased he offered Cody a job as ranch foreman. Cody refused.

He was looking for a more rewarding life; his searching mind was constantly busy absorbing information from the world around him and stimulating him to find new experiences. He could neither read nor write and so to learn, he had to experience life at first-hand without missing any opportunity. He was offered a job by an Englishman, a Mr Blackburn Davis, driving 500 horses first to Galveston, and then sailing with them to London. Each new opportunity his reputation brought him was a challenge and so he set sail to England for the first time.

He delivered the horses to Mr Davis, some to fields beyond Chelsea, and others to a mews in Belgravia. Cody was a strange sight in London, still dressed in his full cowboy regalia – spurs, leather chaps, sombrero and pistol – and he was stared at wherever he went. But Mr Davis's daughter Lela loved his style and his exaggerated courtesies and she showed him the sights. She was an expert horsewoman herself and they rode together many times before he returned to America.

Back in Texas, he could not forget Lela; despite the massive difference in their social positions, he was in love. He made another trip for Mr Davis to deliver horses, but it was really an opportunity to see Lela. On the third trip, he asked her to marry him; she accepted and went with him to a new life in Texas. He had to give up the nomadic life and settle for a job on a ranch so that he could be with her, but he was hopeless with money and the cattle trade was no longer the boom business of the early days. Their life was harsh. Prompted no doubt by dreams of providing a more luxurious life for his wife, his son Leon and another child on the way, when he heard of a gold strike on the Taku Inlet in Alaska nothing Lela could do or say prevented him from joining the Gold Rush. While Samuel Cody went off to a new experience as a gold prospector, Lela, heavily pregnant with their next son, Vivian, made her own way back to her father in England.

It was five years before they saw each other again. In those years he lived a rough and varied life all over the American West. Needless to say he never struck any gold, despite a bitter year in the frozen wilderness of Alaska. He worked his way back to Texas, but there was virtually no work for cowboys. He broke horses for a time but the life no longer stimulated him.

Then, in 1887, he met Adam Forepaugh, the impresario who had shown Cody's namesake, 'Buffalo Bill' Cody, a means to exploit the cowboy legend by turning it into a circus act. Samuel Cody grasped the opportunity with his usual gusto and honed all his newly-obsolete skills to a new perfection for the benefit of paying audiences. He was a natural showman and enjoyed demonstrating feats of marksmanship from the back of a galloping horse. For two years, he toured American cities as 'Captain Cody, King of the Cowboys', gradually earning more money and developing more tricks with gun, whip and horse. By 1889, he was a consummate performer who knew down to the last trick how to hold and thrill an audience. He felt he was ready to start his own show, this time in London, with Lela.

Not only did Lela agree to join the act, she became his human target; her body was surrounded in small glass balls which he shot to pieces with unerring skill. The whole family went on the road; before long, the boys Leon and Vivian, fascinated by the emergence of such a tantalising figure of a father, learned to shoot and joined the act. The Cody family performed in music halls rather than circus rings and together they toured Britain. Then, once again following in Buffalo Bill's footsteps, they toured the Continent. It was the gypsy life again and though Cody dominated his family completely and led them into it, they were quite devoted to him and followed him everywhere.

Cody's magnetic charm and his zest for life held his audiences and made him friends; he had that rare gift of effortlessly transmitting his enthusiasm to others and engaging them with him in a joint enterprise of entertainment or endeavour. He could rarely resist a challenge especially if there was a profit in it: in France and Germany, he rode his horse in races against the top cyclists and invariably won; in Berlin he conducted a horse race down the Unter den Linden for a wager, winning the race and a magnificent horse. In Rome he arranged a chariot race in the Coliseum, dressed in full Roman regalia; bizarre horse races became his stock in trade and he put them on for crowds all over Europe and, in the process, for once made – and kept – a lot of money.

Back in England he returned to the music halls, this time with a play called *The Klondyke Nugget*, a seven-scene melodrama based on the Gold Rush. He devised it himself from his own experiences: there were corrupt sheriffs, Red Indians, plenty of hangings, shootings and opportunities for him to show off his cowboy skills. He painted the scenery, he took the starring role, Lela was the heroine, and when the completed show went on the road in 1899 it was an instant success. Everywhere he took it, it packed the music halls and made the Cody family more money. It was to run without a break for five years.

While *The Klondyke Nugget* payed the bills, Cody had both the time and the resources to indulge in a new idea which had taken hold of his imagination; he had heard reports from South Africa that at the sieges of Ladysmith and Mafeking, the British observation balloons which were used for artillery spotting had been unusable in high winds. To him, the answer was simple: balloons can't fly in high winds but kites love high winds so why not build a man-lifting kite? It was also a challenge.

His knowledge of kites was small and based principally on what he had learnt from a Chinese cook on the long cattle drives in Texas. His knowledge of the science of aeronautics was next to nothing, but he worked things out by common sense and experiment, and then, with his practical skills and inexhaustible energy, he set out to build a man-lifting observation kite for the British Army.

The work went on behind the scenes of *The Klondyke Nugget*: silk was stitched into shape on sewing-machines, bamboo and spruce were cut to size and then, when the weather was right, the whole family would go and try the kite out. Gradually a system developed: he used a pilot kite to take up a light line, then a series of lifter kites to travel up that line, carrying a stronger line. This in turn carried the man-lifting kite under which was slung a wicker basket. It took over a year to perfect the mechanism, trying out different arrangements for the lines which controlled the ascent and descent and different shapes for the kites to keep the whole arrangement stable. When he thought he had got it right, the great day came to try it out.

Cody was the first to go up. First he tested the wind with an anemometer, making sure that it was strong and steady enough to lift him, then he climbed into the wicker basket, his legs poking out through two holes; on his signal, his assistants released the carrier kite, he released the brake on the main line and up he went, as smoothly as in any modern lift. There, the comparison ended: he was out in the open air, a fierce wind singing among the cables which supported him, his legs dangling in mid-air, and he could see for miles around. He came down exhilarated by the experience and warmed by the cheers from the audience which had gathered.

Later that day he went up again to well over a thousand feet. He was thrilled: he had invented a very safe and practical way for the Army to lift men to observe for artillery fire. In 1901, he was granted a provisional patent and then he contacted the War Office and an officer from the Royal Engineers, Major Trollope, was sent to evaluate the system. On a bitter, overcast day, they gave him a demonstration on Holbeck Mow near Leeds; Vivian went up into the clouds with a telephone and came down frozen to the marrow. Trollope was impressed, both by the War Kites, as Cody called them, and by the inventor, and he put in a favourable report to the War Office. The military minds in Whitehall were not as impressed as Major Trollope and in any case, the Boer War was over. They did nothing, but that demonstration was the beginning of a long and very curious relationship between the bureaucratic and aloof British military Establishment and the flamboyant cowboy/showman/inventor who was to become their first pilot.

Having invested a great deal of money in his kites and real-ising their crowd-pulling potential, Cody put them to commercial use. Wherever *The Klondyke Nugget* was performed the kites would be flown near the town and they were a great success in drawing crowds. He branched out into other areas too, using them for meteorological experiments and achieving a world height record of 14,000 feet, and in 1902 he was made a Fellow of the Royal Meteorological Society. But he still wanted to use his kites for military observation and was determined to try again, this time with the Admiralty.

The Royal Navy invited him down to Portsmouth to give a demonstration, first on land and then at sea. Whatever first impression officers and men had of their flamboyant kite-man with his shoulder-length hair, his sombrero and cowboy boots,

Cody was always able to win their attention by his charm and a little showmanship. But to military men it was his personal example of utter fearlessness which won their affection. On one test, he was being towed behind a destroyer when the captain turned through 180 degrees, leaving him without enough wind to fly. A quick-thinking officer cut the kite free of the ship and Cody started a rapid descent from 800 feet, swinging like a pendulum beneath the lifter kites. He waited until he was about thirty feet above the water, then, at the end of a swing, at the point where the basket was stationary, he leapt free into the sea. But whatever impression he made on the sailors, the Admiralty were unimpressed and declined just as the Army had done.

In 1903 Cody once again turned his inventions to civilian use, which also served as a means of publicising them: he crossed the Channel at night, in thirteen hours, in a small boat drawn by kites. He was a popular figure and such feats of daring won him national acclaim. He was a frequent visitor to the Royal Aeronautical Society where he exchanged views with the aeronautical luminaries of the day, but when his friend, the Hon. Charles Rolls, put him up for membership of the Royal Aero Club, he was rejected by the committee. In Britain, aeronautics was a social or sporting pastime for the wealthy; playboy balloonists, generals and admirals could not conceive how a contrivance such as a kite, flown by a bizarre music-hall artiste, could be of any aeronautical or military value.

Cody was anxious to leave the stage and take up aeronautics full-time, but he had to make a living and provide for his family. His mind was moving towards powered flight. From his captive kite, he wanted to develop a free-flying glider then, by powering it, he would develop an aeroplane.

The Army unwittingly helped Cody to fulfil his dream. They appointed a Colonel Capper as Superintendent of the Balloon Factory at Farnborough and the colonel knew Major Trollope who had told him all about Cody and his kites.

Colonel Capper was one of the visionaries who could see that the air would soon be conquered and that the first practical use of flying machines would be for military observation. He lobbied the War Office to let him carry out some trials with Cody and his kites; he also wanted to find out if Cody could be useful in other aeronautical experiments. The trials were a great success and Capper strongly recommended that the War Office buy a set of kites and employ Cody as Chief Instructor for three months at a salary of £55 a month. Two months later the War Office agreed.

The lifestyle of the Cody family changed dramatically: they took a house in Sydenham, their youngest son Frank went to a local boarding school, and the whole family gave up the stage and took a large cut in income as a result. Cody was determined that his engagement as the Army's Kiting Instructor should last longer than three months and also serve as a springboard for his other aeronautical ambitions. Though he was officially employed by the Army, he continued to dress like a cowboy, his hair remained long, and when out instructing he rode a large grey horse named Bergamo and frequently gave the soldiers a taste of his skills as a marksman and as a showman. He was a very round peg fitting snugly into a very square hole.

With Capper's connivance, his contract was renewed several times until 1906, when he was given a yearly contract at £1000 a year plus expenses, including free fodder for Bergamo. But though they kept up the pretence that Cody was fully employed as a Kiting Instructor, the two men were really working on other aeronautical projects which they felt certain would eventually be much more useful.

There were two other projects under way at Farnborough while Cody was there. He worked on the engine nacelles and later flew in Britain's first airships, the *Nulli Secundus* 1 and 2. But airships were a diversion; he was more interested in the second project, the aeroplane.

It would be harsh to describe Colonel Capper as a spy, but he visited the Wright Brothers in Dayton in 1905 ostensibly to discuss the possible purchase of an aeroplane but with the express purpose of learning more about their methods. His relations with the Wright Brothers were very cordial, but he never really intended to provide a channel for the Wrights to sell their aircraft in Britain. Though Cody benefited from the information which Capper brought back, he had his own way of experimenting and he stuck to it. The Wrights were scientific; he was much more empirical. He did develop a glider and he powered it too, but the powered version was never big enough to carry a man. By the summer of 1908, British Army Aeroplane No. 1 was ready to fly but the only engine the Army possessed, the Antoinette, was in the airship *Nulli Secundus* 2. So it was not until the autumn that he got the chance to carry out some powered ground runs, then some short hops culminating in the triumph of 16 October.

Cody's aircraft of 1908 was a remarkable achievement, even though it crashed. Early in 1909 it was ready again, this time with a host of modifications including a wing-warping system, larger propellers and an array of streamers attached to the rear of the wings so that observers could see the airflow. On 20 January he flew again and crashed again.

Just as Cody was closest to the success he had so diligently pursued on behalf of the War Office, the bureaucrats dealt him the cruellest blow they could – they sacked him. The cruelty could be forgiven if there was a good reason, but Cody was sacked out of muddled thinking and ignorance. The Committee for Imperial Defence sat in 1908 to consider the future of military aviation. Even after Wilbur's display and the achievements of other aviators in France, and after Cody's own flight that October, the Committee decided that there was no future for heavier-than-air machines and consequently no reason to continue employing Cody. In April 1909, he was given notice of six months, but he chose not to serve it and left immediately. The stupidity of the officials was at least consistent; since they had decided that they had no use for aeroplanes, when he asked if he could keep Army Aeroplane No. 1, they agreed, and even lent him the Antoinette engine. Curiously, they also let him continue experimenting over Laffan's Plain, part of the old Farnborough Common, and he built a shed on the far side and began a new career – that of independent, freelance aircraft constructor.

Unfettered by bureaucracy, Cody's mind was given a new lease of creative freedom. Spurred on by the *Daily Mail*'s offer of a prize of £1000 for the first circular, one-mile flight by a British subject, in a British-made aircraft, he began rebuilding his aeroplane under a new name – Cody Biplane No. 1.

One of his first outings in it was a piece of pure Cody showmanship: the Army was conducting manoeuvres nearby and the Prince and Princess of Wales were in attendance. He made a couple of passes over the troops who stopped to wave and cheer, disrupting their training; later the same day he took off and flew in a straight line for a mile – a British record.

The Royal couple came to visit him and asked him to repeat the performance; he was delighted to oblige, though the flight ended in a minor crash on landing. He went on improving the design and, before long, he managed a circular flight of over two miles but because he was still an American citizen and the engine was French he could not qualify for the £1000 prize.

In August 1909, the month of the great aviation show at Rheims and only weeks after Blériot had flown the Channel, Cody took his friend Colonel Capper for a two-mile flight over Laffan's Plain. This would surely change the Army's attitude! He then took his wife for a flight, and so the long-suffering Lela became the first woman to fly in the British Empire and the United States. By this time, he had returned the Army's Antoinette engine and installed a more powerful ENV which had improved the performance of his big aircraft a great deal.

But there was still little military interest in the Cody No. 1, and so its inventor turned once again to show-business: the city of Doncaster decided to hold the first flying display in Britain and Cody was invited to take part. He knew the value of his aeroplane as a crowd-puller and demanded £2000 for the show. Another town, Blackpool, entered the fray, but while they made up their minds, Cody signed up with Doncaster with an advance of £500. The Aero Club threatened to ban any pilot who took part in the Doncaster display but Cody, though now a member, ignored them. He had a mishap on the ground and only managed some short flights, but he thrilled the crowd in another way: with the Doncaster Civic Band in attendance and before a crowd of thousands, Samuel F. Cody, Texas cowboy, music-hall artiste and aeronautical pioneer, became a British subject, signing the papers on the back of the Town Clerk to the cheers of his new countrymen. He was now eligible to enter for the *Daily Mail* prize.

He did not win the prize, he was just beaten to it by J. T. Moore-Brabazon flying a Wright *Flyer* built under licence by Short Brothers using the only home-built engine available at the time.

As an independent constructor, Cody pursued his own individual line. There was a new wave of pioneer pilots in the fray now: Geoffrey De Havilland, T. O. M. Sopwith, Handley Page, and A. V. Roe. And there was fierce competition to build and sell aircraft, especially to the Army. Cody's aircraft reflected his character; they were large, robust, elegant and beautifully finished and they were nicknamed 'Flying Cathedrals'. He flew them with the flamboyance of a showman, and the instinctive poise and balance of a cowboy: straight and level one minute and turning over a sixpence the next.

Finally, the Army realised that it was going to have to come to terms with the military potential of aircraft and in 1912, Military Trials were held on Salisbury Plain with cash prizes of many thousands of pounds. Cody nearly missed the Trials; he had planned to take two aircraft but just weeks before the most important date in the aviation calendar, he crashed them both. To start with, he was desolate, but he set to and with the help of his sons, a few employees and some who helped simply because it was

Cody who needed them, he rebuilt the biplane, now called the Cody V, and had it ready just in time.

The tests in the Trials were very exacting: climbing tests, gliding tests, duration tests, oil- and fuel-consumption tests. There was scrutiny from the ground and each pilot was obliged to carry an officer of the Royal Flying Corps as official observer. The competition from home and abroad was fierce too: Blériot, Breguet, Deperdussin and Hanriot were there from France and most of the British industry were in contention to sell military aircraft to the biggest empire in the world.

The weather for the trials was awful; it was cloudy and drizzly. The field was gradually whittled down, but Cody hung on through his own toughness and his shrewd tactics, never flying when the weather was too bad, never risking his one and only machine. On the ground he was his usual gregarious self, a mixture of friendliness to all, showmanship and engaging conversation. In the air he was cool, crafty and superb as a pilot; he was soon favourite in the British Section. The French machines dominated the International Section, but he kept plugging away, and through his doggedness and deft handling, and through the strength and performance of his old biplane, he gradually crushed the opposition. He won both Sections outright and carried off £5000 in prize money and an order for two of his aircraft for the RFC.

There was no doubt about his win, the rules were too strict for any errors, but the Cody V was really very old-fashioned by 1912 and it won mainly through Cody's own expert handling. The Trials did not help the Army very much, and eventually the RFC bought a variety of aircraft to try out.

But Cody was back on top, at the very peak of his career, and the money and the success only spurred him on again. He was intent on a new goal – not just to be a famous pilot, but to be a serious manufacturer as well. He became a pillar of the mainstream of British aviation. In the early days, the illiterate Cody had attended lectures at the Royal Aeronautical Society, where he had listened and learnt; now he went there to lecture in his modified Texas drawl.

He set about forming a company – Cody & Sons Aerial Navigation. Vivian married one of the girls who had sewn fabric for them since the early Farnborough days, and Leon and Frank were as keen as ever. The *Daily Mail* had offered a prize of £5000 for a coastal race round Britain; in 1913, the same paper offered a £10,000 prize for a crossing of the Atlantic. The Codys were stirred by prizes, it kept them in the limelight and kept the money coming in and provided them with an outlet for their natural showmanship. They started work on a seaplane, bigger than the *Cathedral*, and aimed at the coastal race.

The Cody VI was his last aeroplane. At the peak of his success, and with who knows what possibilities still to come from his fertile mind, the seaplane broke up on a joy ride with the Hampshire cricket captain on board; both men fell out from 250 feet and were killed instantly. Cody was fifty-two.

Lela, his family, his hundreds of friends and thousands of admirers, were devastated. His funeral was a spectacle of which he would have been proud: whole regiments of the British Army turned out from Aldershot not on orders, but as volunteers; his body was carried on a gun carriage draped in the Union Jack and drawn by the Royal Engineers; 50,000 people lined the route to the Military Cemetery and he became the first civilian to be buried there.

Cody's life had been spent unconsciously winning affection. With his death, there was an outpouring of genuine grief from high and low: the King sent a personal telegram of condolence to Lela; the War Office was represented at the funeral, as was the Admiralty and Parliament; thousands of soldiers saluted the grave and the flowers had to be transported in lorries, one wreath from the girls at the local telephone exchange remembering his never-failing courtesy on the line. It was the grandest funeral a Texas cowboy ever had.

He was the powerhouse of the Cody family and with his death, Cody aviation ended. Only Frank, who had seen his father fall to his death, took to the air as a pilot; he was killed in aerial combat in the RFC in 1917. Vivian remained at Farnborough, becoming head of the Fabric Shop, and died in 1961; Leon served in the Royal Navy with kites and balloons and died during the Second World War. Lela died in 1939 and was buried beside her husband at Aldershot.

There are two strange memorials to Samuel Cody. The first is an aluminium casting of a dead tree which stands inside the fence at Farnborough. In the early days, when the tree was alive, Cody used to tie his aeroplane to it and run the engines up to full power to test them; it was preserved as a memorial until it had nearly rotted away, when the casting was made. The second memorial is more controversial and on one occasion caused the plaque on the tree to be changed. In 1948, a former railway booking clerk and devoted follower and helper of Cody, G. A. Broomfield, wrote a book called *Pioneer of the Air*. He claimed that Cody had flown in May 1908, five months before he actually did. Cody could not possibly have done so, for the only engine available at the time, the Antoinette, was in the airship *Nulli Secundus* and there are documents which show that Cody was away with the Navy that month. Broomfield made the claim in an effort to ensure that the hops, for they were no more than that, which A. V. Roe made in July 1908, would not knock his beloved Cody off his perch as the first pilot to fly in Britain. He need not have worried for reasons which will become apparent in the next chapter.

Let the book stand, with its inaccuracies, not as a testimony to Cody the airman, but to the affection which he generated in people and to one man's regard for him.

4   Sir Alliott Verdon-Roe

It promised to be a jewel of a summer's day. A red and golden sun sparkled between the chimney-pots and slate roofs of East London and lightened the sky to powder blue. On 13 July 1909, at 5.00 a.m., the world belonged to anybody who was up and about with the senses to taste it; the streets were empty, the air was still and clean and the background bustle of the city had yet to erupt. It was a day for nothing but optimism and hope.

Alliott Verdon-Roe loved the early morning. He cycled out beyond the houses, following the railway-lines across the green strip of marshland where the River Lea runs through Hackney. There was no wind, the atmosphere was damp and the whiff of goats and donkeys hung around the red-brick railway embankment where he dismounted and parked his bike. He unlocked one of the boarded-up arches, opened up the improvised doors and let the new day in to warm the dark interior.

The sunlight fell on A. V. Roe's most prized possession, an aeroplane of simple but exquisite construction: spindly wooden struts between wings made of tarred paper, braced with a spider's-web of piano wire around a triangular fuselage shaped rather like a canoe. The tiny 9-hp JAP engine and the four-bladed propeller were out in front and behind them there was just room for a pilot cockpit amidships. The intricate construction which looked dangerously delicate was, once again in this pioneering age, the product of a single, very individual mind; a mind of relentless inventiveness directed unashamedly in the pursuit of simplicity and practicality. The whole machine weighed around 200 lbs. (It can be seen today suspended from the ceiling of the Science Museum in London.)

Several days previously Roe had crashed it, but now, after many hours of work, he was ready to try again. His faithful band of helpers arrived, most of them by bike, and they gingerly wheeled the aircraft out to a clear patch of ground between a fence and the River Lea. Some of them then took up tools and spares and one mounted a bicycle, clutching a fire extinguisher, ready to chase the aircraft and douse the fires which they had now come to expect when Roe crashed.

Satisfied that every adjustment had been made, he climbed into the little cockpit. The only instruments were a throttle and a stick with a crosspiece which simultaneously controlled the warping by turning it and the elevator by pulling and pushing on it. He opened the throttle; the engine popped and banged and the whole structure shook as it sped over the ground on two bicycle wheels. Gradually the shaking subsided; the weight was transferring from the wheels to the straining wings; slowly, the ride became smoother and smoother until an end to the rumbling told the pilot that he was airborne. The flight was a wallowing one, but as he eased back on the stick, so it climbed to about ten feet and remained airborne for just over thirty yards, coming down in one piece.

The helpers rushed up to the landing-site only seconds after the aircraft, thrilled now that there was no mishap to deal with. Roe climbed out, his natural smiling face beaming with pleasure. It was the first ever flight of any distance to be made in Britain, by a British national, in a British aircraft, with a British engine.

The date was just less than a fortnight before Blériot's flight across the Channel so radically changed attitudes to aviation in Britain, for even as the flight was made, the local council was taking court proceedings to stop Roe experimenting over common land.

Brushes with the authorities were nothing new to A. V. Roe. He was a quiet, self-effacing man who frequently suffered at the hands of blustering, self-important officials. Like the Wright Brothers (whom he admired greatly), he could not project himself forcefully among the Establishment figures of the day; he was given virtually no support and had to rely on his wits both to find the resources to build his machines in the first place, and then to stay ahead of the short-sighted officials who tried to stop him experimenting.

The Lea Marshes were far from ideal as an airfield. Space was severely limited and the ground was rough, but it was about the only place A. V. (as he was to be universally known) could find. He had been unceremoniously evicted from his early experimental area at the Brooklands motor-racing circuit; the local authorities refused him permission both at Wimbledon Common and Wormwood Scrubs and when he had approached the War Office to see if he could build a shed alongside Cody's at Farnborough, they too refused. (Roe was very bitter about this decision since

Cody was at that time an American, a freelance and engaged on the same line of research.)

The early years of his experimental life were dogged by lack of funds, lack of support, crushing rebuffs at the hands of the aeronautical Establishment, especially the military, and yet his flair for design, combined with his engineering genius, turned out some of the best ideas with some of the best military aircraft of all time.

In the days before the Ship Canal brought industry into the heart of Manchester, the area around Trafford Park was a solid belt of Victorian middle-class prosperity. Business and professional men built the dream homes of the time there; big, formal houses widely spaced along wide, leafy roads with plenty of room for large families, servants and horses.

In just such a house, called The Poplars, in Patricroft, Alliott Verdon-Roe was born on 26 April 1877. His father was a doctor and he and his gentle wife ran the household on classic Victorian lines: strictness of behaviour mellowed by a progressive interest in new ideas; thrift and accountability mellowed by more-than-ritual charity and good works. Mrs Sofia Verdon-Roe (Verdon was her maiden name) had seven children, though one had died; Alliott was the fourth. Alongside her own children, she founded and ran an orphanage nearby and when the family moved to London she founded another in Putney.

When he was eight, Alliott and his younger brother Humphrey were sent to a preparatory school called Haliford House near Brooklands. Life at a boarding school of the 1880s was not the environment to bring out the best of the Verdon-Roe boys. They had inherited their mother's gentleness of spirit and were natural targets for all the bullies such a system could muster. They went through three preparatory schools, Haliford House, Shorne College and Bewshers; except for sport, 'Roe Major's' only memorable achievements were fights, being sent to Coventry and getting caned. He went on to St Paul's but he could not find any enthusiasm for academic subjects and, sport aside, his only interest was in technical drawing. At fourteen he was getting nowhere. So, despite Alliott's tender years and despite his own ambitions that his son would become a doctor, when a family friend offered to teach A. V. surveying in Canada, his father sent him off alone by steamer, across the Atlantic, then right across the continent by train to British Columbia. His schooldays were over.

It was an invigorating adventure for such a young man and he flourished, quickly adapting to the self-sufficient lifestyle. There was little work for surveyors, so he turned his hands to anything to make a living: fishing, tree-planting and franking the mail in the Balfour Post Office. It was a life which demanded thrift even to survive, yet in a few months, he had managed to save $50 out of his wages and bought a half-share in two plots of land. In what spare time he had, he studied engineering theory from books. In 1893, when his year in Canada was up, he went back to England, much matured and determined to become an engineer.

The Roes had moved to London, but A. V. went back to Lancashire, to be apprenticed to the Lancashire and Yorkshire Railway Locomotive Works at Horwich. He was still only sixteen, but he led a busy and independent life, living in digs, getting to work by six every morning and filling his few recreational hours and weekends cycle-racing. Cycling became something of an obsession and it was to last all his life, but in those youthful days he was a champion. He turned many of his prizes into cash, always adding to his savings. His bike saved him money too: once, he cycled home to London in twenty-two hours to see his parents. At work, he found other ways to earn money: his wages were based on a certain output with extra for work produced above the fixed rate. He simplified the process of starting and stopping his lathe by attaching lines to the overhead handles which started and stopped it, so shortening the operating-time and regularly earning him time-and-a-half. His savings grew.

In 1898 he finished his apprenticeship. So, with a sound basic knowledge of engineering, a host of certificates and a desire to travel, he decided to join the Royal Navy. After more study at King's College, London, he sat the exam. He passed the technical papers but was still turned down. Perhaps the Royal Navy had no place for an officer of such gentle and independent spirit.

Still looking for a means to travel, he joined the Merchant Navy as a fifth engineer; he took his bike to sea with him to travel inland from the ports he visited. His duties never fully occupied his busy mind on the long days at sea; he was constantly looking around for outlets for his bubbling inventiveness, usually by designing or improving a simple gadget to solve a problem or overcome an inconvenience. And his inquisitiveness was not limited to engineering: from the deck of the SS *Inchanga*, in the balmy Southern Ocean, he spent hours observing the serene and majestic flight of an albatross which teamed up with the ship. The mariners' greatest friend is superbly equipped to glide: long, efficient wings with flight and control feathers. If the albatross could fly, why not man? How to build a suitable apparatus? It was the same questions that had stirred the Wrights.

He started his research by constructing a model albatross out of wood and attempting to glide it on the ship. It flew very badly, but it amused the rest of the crew immensely. With his basic engineering skills, with what he read about flight and aeronautics and by persistent trial and error, he gradually built up a store of knowledge and steadily improved his models. He tried canard types, monoplanes, biplanes, triplanes, multiplanes and tandem-winged planes.

At home between voyages, his research continued; he took the models up to the highest window in his father's house and launched them into the garden below. Once again there was an audience: the inmates of a nursing home next-door complained that the Roe house was a lunatic asylum where the inmates spent the entire day throwing things out of the windows.

By 1902 aeronautics had gripped him. After the tedium of seven trips to the Russian oil port of Batoum, A. V. decided to give up the sea and concentrate on aviation full-time. He had his savings, but he took a job as a draughtsman in the motorcar industry, designing gearbox systems and at the same time reading tirelessly about aeronautics and experimenting with models.

In December 1903, he heard about the Wright Brothers' flights at Kitty Hawk and, unlike most European experimenters, he was neither piqued nor dismissive. He wrote to Wilbur and told him of his own experiments and Wilbur, who sensed a fellow 'airman' (not to mention cyclist), replied very cordially and with encouragement, though without giving away any of his own methods. Two years later, in January 1906, A. V. publicly declared his faith in the claims of the Wright Brothers and set out his own ideas about flight in a letter to *The Times*, putting his own view that powered flight was a reality and that he intended to research in the same area. It was published, but not without this sour and patronising note by the Engineering Editor: 'It is not to be supposed that we can in any way adopt the writer's estimate of his undertaking, being of the opinion, indeed, that all attempts at artificial aviation on the basis he describes are not only dangerous to human life but foredoomed to failure from an engineering standpoint.'

Three years after the Kitty Hawk flights, Britain was asleep; A. V. and the tiny band of 'airmen' in Britain could find virtually no support.

The following year, the *Daily Mail* announced a competition.

Lord Northcliffe offered £250 in prizes for model aeroplanes capable of mechanical flight. There were around two hundred model entries but there were a whole host of other exhibits which had nothing to do with mechanical flight at all. A. V. entered three models; one was an eight-foot wingspan biplane with a pusher propeller and an elevator at the front. It was powered by elastic and on the day of the competition it was in a class of its own: it flew the furthest distance possible inside the hall at Alexandra Palace, and outside it flew well over a hundred feet. Nothing else came near it and A. V. was a clear and outright winner. The judges, however, were 'unsatisfied', none of the models had performed well enough in their view to justify the first prize of £150, so they awarded A. V. just £75.

There was another crushing blow to come from the Aero Club judges; their eyes alighted on an exhibit which neither flew nor could fly. Short Brothers had displayed some beautiful spliced-rope- and basket-weaving aimed at the ballooning fraternity and the Gold Medal was awarded to them. The Silver Medal went to a contraption under a glass case designed around two electroplated glass bowls and some beautifully polished cogwheels; A. V. was told that the award was for 'workmanship'. The Bronze Medal went to a postman for a silk and bamboo feather attached to a crank which beat the air and created a draught.

A. V. was inwardly very bitter about the awards and he remembered the miscarriage of justice all his life. His own account of the competition shows he took it personally; he was a sensitive man with a very simple belief in justice and to be brushed aside so peremptorily by his 'betters' really hurt. But he never let it show; the photograph of him with his model has his perpetual grin.

It is very easy to be cynical and disparaging about the attitudes which prevailed in the British aeronautical Establishment at the time. With the benefit of reading A. V.'s own account of his experiences, many other historical accounts, and eighty years of hindsight, it is easy to cast aspersions; the plain fact is, however, that those who set themselves up as patrons of aviation, many of whom had the resources to experiment seriously, could not see where to go. They based their judgements on prejudice against the 'airman' concept of flight; it demanded an intricate, practical understanding of science and engineering which the sportsmen and playboys of the day neither had, nor wished to acquire. Their minds conceived balloons and airships, sedate, even grand machines patrolling the Empire like ocean liners and providing facilities more in keeping with their lifestyle.

Airships like the *Nulli Secundus*, which Cody was working on at the time, found favour with the authorities; with his natural rapport and gift of showmanship, he charmed his way into a position where he could do the research he wanted to do on aeroplanes at the War Office's expense. When he was summarily dismissed, he thrived on the challenge thrown up by the perversity of officials and decision-makers. A. V., on the other hand, bore it stoically and suffered quietly.

Whatever the differences in their characters, both men were seekers after truth, scientific truth, born out of practical experiment and demonstration; the lack of confidence in his models shown by the judges of the *Daily Mail*'s competition did nothing to blunt A. V.'s confidence, even if his pride and sense of justice had been damaged.

Before the end of 1907 A. V. had embarked on his dream of a powered aircraft which would carry a man. The owners of Brooklands motor-racing circuit had offered a prize of £2500 for a flight round the circuit before the end of the year and since A. V. had difficulty finding anywhere to experiment, he asked if he could do so at the circuit. He was allowed to put up a shed next to the finishing straight but there were rules imposed by an aggressive and unsympathetic manager: he was not allowed to sleep in his shed so, each night, he bade goodnight to the gatekeeper and climbed back over the wall; there was a fence between the shed and the track and he was refused permission to make a section of it detachable, but he went ahead and did so anyway, making the join so neatly that nobody ever knew since he removed it very early in the mornings. On one occasion, when the track was using his shed for refreshments, the manager ordered some of his men to move A. V.'s aircraft and in doing so they damaged it badly. It was a tough life: he cooked his own food and lived on dates, kippers and bacon, for which he allowed himself around five shillings a week; the winter of 1907–8 was a bitterly cold one and at night he could not light his coke fire for fear that this might give away his presence.

His first aircraft was a biplane with front elevator but the 9-hp JAP engine he had at the time was not powerful enough to get it off the ground. He managed to fly it at Brooklands by getting sympathetic motorists to tow him. It was a hair-raising method of getting airborne; sometimes the motorists held on too long, and once, he landed on the spiked railings of the fence, but these towed hops proved to him that he had got the principles right and gave him valuable experience at the controls. In the spring of 1908, he managed to borrow a French engine, one of the famous Antoinettes; by June he was getting the wheels off the ground, but then the blow fell. The Brooklands management gave him notice to quit; he had nowhere to go and so was forced to sell his shed to them for £15. He never won the £2500 prize.

Not only did he need a new flying ground, he also wanted to start from scratch again on his design. He was now more than ever convinced that the 'tail first' designs of the Wrights and Cody were not the soundest way to fly and so he worked on the 'tractor' configuration, with the propeller in front, which was to be so successful.

After a round of refusals from the local authorities of nearly all the open spaces around London, he settled on the Lea Marshes, initially because they were open to the public, but also because he could rent a railway arch nearby. He moved there early in 1909 and with the dedicated band of followers which had gathered around him he began building the triplane. The Antoinette engine had had to go back to its owner in France and so he was back to the JAP, but with the wonderfully light machine which he now designed, he triumphed in July that year.

In 1909 Wilbur Wright visited France again to demonstrate his *Flyers*. A. V. wanted to see the aircraft at first-hand and meet Wilbur, so he got on his bike and cycled all the way to Le Mans via Southampton. Wilbur had been pestered by numerous people, nobility, royalty even, to let them see the *Flyer*, and by that time he was fed up with answering the same silly questions over and over again and, characteristically, saw very few people. With A. V. it was different: he was pleased to see him, first because he was a serious fellow aviator (and cyclist) who knew what he was talking about and asked sensible questions, and secondly because he above all remembered A. V. from his letter in 1903 and the acceptance and support he had voiced at the time. They had a friendly and invigorating exchange of ideas, then Wilbur drove A. V. and his bike back into the town of Le Mans where they parted; A. V. then cycled back to London through the night, stopping only to quaff cider offered by a French farmer.

The same year A. V. flew the triplane on home ground at the Air Meet at Blackpool, but he could only manage a few 'straights' and he won no prizes. Most of his savings had disappeared into his aircraft and he lagged behind most of the other competitors because he could not afford a powerful enough engine. Not only that, his wings were covered in yellow oilpaper instead of fabric; it softened in the damp atmosphere of Blackpool and sagged between the formers of the wings, earning him the nickname 'Yellow Peril'. When he wanted to use lightweight steel tubing in the aircraft and discovered that it would cost ten pounds, he left the dealer's yard crestfallen, cycled to a timberyard in Wandsworth and made do with wood instead which cost only a few shillings. His problem was money; his savings had run out; what he lacked was proper financial backing.

His father, somehow reconciled to his son's success in the non-existent profession of aeronautics, lent him a little money but it was his younger brother, Humphrey, with whom he had shared those depressing schooldays, who really came to the rescue and became the financial architect of A. V. Roe & Co Ltd., later known across the world by the acronym Avro.

Humphrey, or H. V. as he was inevitably known, had embarked on a career as a soldier and fought through the Boer War. He had given up the Army in 1902 and taken over a firm of webbing manufacturers, Everard & Co., on the death of a great-uncle who had owned it. By 1909 he was an experienced businessman and went into partnership with A. V. A. V. was the designer/ constructor/pilot and H. V. was the manager/organiser and financier. They tried to interest outside parties in investing in the firm but without success so, with the goodwill of their mother, who had every confidence in H. V.'s business head, and a little more money from their somewhat hesitant father, on New Year's Day 1910 they gave up trying to attract sponsors and went their own way. It was 1912 before there was any return on the capital and by that time H. V. had invested £10,000.

Avro progressed slowly but steadily; the experimental work was carried on at a revitalised Brooklands, where the new management had now encouraged aircraft builders to congregate. The accounts were kept in Manchester, alongside those of Everard & Co. Eventually, the manufacturing of aircraft was established there too. A. V. was now able to afford more powerful engines and redesign his aircraft, sticking to his favoured tractor design but concentrating on a biplane rather than a triplane. By 1913, this new line of thinking produced the prototype of one of the most successful aircraft of all time – the Avro 504.

The 504 is a legend, a thoroughbred A. V. design. It was a rather large, two-cockpit biplane with dual controls and a rotary engine; it had a finesse and lightness in both concept and engineering which made it easier to handle than most contemporary aircraft. When war came in 1914, the 504 became the standard training aircraft of the RFC and it revolutionised pilot training. Up to that time, pilots were trained in a fairly haphazard way: the instructor would brief his pupil on the ground, take him for a few rides in a single-control aircraft such as a Maurice Farman Longhorn and then send him off solo. If the pupil survived, and could execute a certain number of manoeuvres, often observed from the ground, he got a certificate. The architect of the revolution, the man who gave the world proper pilot training, was the commander of the School of Special Flying at Gosport, Lieutenant Colonel Smith-Barry. But without the 504 as a basic training machine, rather than the B.E.s produced by the government factory at Farnborough, his task would have been very much more difficult.

Once the official designers got their hands on the 504 it was steadily modified by committee, and gradually became more and more a hotchpotch of design ideas and less of a single, finely-engineered machine. For example, when a new engine mounting had to be designed, to take a more powerful engine, A. V. managed to design a lightweight plate to support it but the officials rejected his ideas in favour of a plate of twice the weight. A. V. argued plaintively and vainly against the 'experts'. He simply did not have the forcefulness of personality to push through his own designs against those in authority whose ideas conflicted with his.

The 504 was not a fighting aircraft (though it was a flight of 504s who carried out the first bombing raid on the Zeppelin works at Friedrichshafen in November 1914) so it was never lavished with the heroic qualities of the Sopwith Camel, the Bristol Fighter and the S.E.5a, but its contribution to the air war was nevertheless immense. Avro in Manchester produced about ten thousand 504s, and around the same number were produced by other firms under licence; and some examples were still flying in the RAF in the early 1930s, heavily modified though still at heart the product of A. V.'s mind, hand and eye.

Smith-Barry, an honest man who occasionally suffered for his outspokenness, had no doubts about where the best of the 504s came from. He felt the touch of a genius in A. V.'s aircraft and said so, also saying that they were better than all their rivals. He felt they came from nature and likened them to birds, giving the pilot no more a sense of being aware of his wings than a bird is.

During the Great War A. V.'s restless mind, though concentrating on the detail of aircraft design, ranged into many areas; he was never a simple technocrat or obsessive engineer. The main Avro factory was in Manchester but A. V. had a dream to create a new and modern works on the South Coast, combined with an idyllic garden city for the workforce nearby, where they 'could breathe

God's fresh air'. He had other visions, too, that after the war long-range flying boats would link up the Empire and that Avro would produce them, not in Manchester, but on the South Coast. He got as far as buying a green site with a mile or so of foreshore on the Hamble River opposite Southampton and making a start on his experimental works and some of the houses. Unfortunately shortage of building materials caused by the war brought the project to a halt and after the war the slump in the aircraft industry meant that the scheme was financially impossible.

He had a vision of a time after the war when aviation would be used to improve communications and become a potent force in the world. Avro was one of the first aircraft manufacturers to take on aeronautical apprentices to provide a backbone of skilled men on the shop floor. A. V. was not a man to whom levels of social standing meant anything; he was extremely friendly to men on the shop floor and they returned that affection. The main purpose in his life was in designing and improving products and he was always in the factory himself, explaining, discussing his ideas with his staff.

Alliott Verdon-Roe was an idealist and, like many idealists, he was overtaken by the harsh realities of a troubled world which more pragmatic and aggressive people understand and organise.

When the doldrums hit the aircraft industry after the war Avro diversified into motorcars, taking over the Crossley firm. The businessman brother, H. V., was no longer with the firm (he had fought in the war in the RFC and afterwards married the sociologist and pioneer of contraception, Dr Marie Stopes, and did not wish to go back into business). Some aircraft manufacturers ceased to operate their businesses, mothballing them until a rearmament programme would mean more orders, but A. V. soldiered on with his beloved firm, designing cars and motorcycles and a unique 'monocar', a sort of motorcycle with a bucket seat and a windscreen. Such innovations were not fashionable and shares in the firm declined steadily; by the late 1920s market forces had beaten him and he was forced to sell. The huge assets of Avro, not just the works, but many of the designs and patents which it held, were taken over by the giant armaments conglomerate, Sir W. G. Armstrong-Whitworth Ltd., which was then headed by a rising star of the business world, John Siddeley.

A. V. was bitter about the takeover; he saw the firm which he and his family had started with a pittance, and which had money ploughed back into it year after year, whipped away from him. It was another example of the unfairness of the system. With his liberal ideas, the shock of the loss of his firm made him think about the business and financial system: he rejected the Socialist answer, but earnestly pursued monetary reform, believing that the banks had too much power through their ability to effectively create money by the issue of cheques and credit and that that power should properly be vested in the state. For the rest of his life, he lobbied politicians on money reform and anybody else who would listen.

Even as he lost control of Avro, the Establishment was about to deal him another cruel blow. A dinner was held to commemorate his flight at Brooklands on 8 June 1908 but it sparked off a controversy about who was the first Englishman to fly in England. The Royal Aero Club set up a Committee to decide on the matter, and it ruled that A. V.'s flight was not a proper flight. Instead, the honour was bestowed upon J. T. Moore-Brabazon for a flight in a Voisin biplane the following year. Brabazon was a tireless promoter of aviation and, after a youthful flirtation with balloons, an airman of distinction. Without detracting from him as an aviator in any way, the plain fact is that he was never a pioneer in the conceiver/designer/builder/pilot sense, in the way that A. V. was; he was, however, one of the earliest members of the Aero Club. Once again there was a consolation prize for A.V., though this time not one in the gift of the Club. In 1929, he became, some might argue rather belatedly, Sir Alliott Verdon-Roe.

Freed from the financial headaches in Manchester, A. V. pursued his other dream in aviation – flying boats. An old friend and colleague, John Lord, left Avro with him and together they acquired a controlling interest in a boat-building firm, S. E. Saunders, in Cowes; they had built 504s during the war under contract. A series of 'Saro' flying boats came from the factory: the *London*, the *Lerwick*, and culminating in the *Princess*, a ten-engined monster designed for the post-World War Two long-distance routes. It was another dream which never really came true, for though they were masterpieces of design and construction, long-distance passengers wanted the speed and comfort of the new jets like the Comet and the Boeing 707.

A. V. died in 1958. Right up to the end of his life he kept designing and improving: all-round bumpers for cars, flush push-button doorhandles, headlamps with glasses at the side to avoid dazzle were added to his collection of patents and ideas; this had started when he was thirteen with a hairbrush with a reversible head to lengthen the life of the bristles and included a flattened steel spring to replace the whalebone in ladies' corsets. And there was also the bicycle to go on improving; he designed a frame for use by either men or women with tubes of varying diameter according to the load which was put on them, thereby lightening it and strengthening it. No problem was too great or too small for him to put his mind to: a trouser press made light enough to travel with; detailed plans for a model industrial city.

And he remained thrifty, a lifelong trait with origins right back in his childhood. His son Royce remembers him leaving for work each day, as chairman of the board, with a tin of Marmite sandwiches and how he preferred a car which could free-wheel to save petrol.

Sir Alliott Verdon-Roe had one of the most inventive minds this century and with his inventiveness came a vision of how life could be improved by technology. But he was an idealist and a practical visionary without the hardness of character or the personality to drive through the opposing arguments. Put simply, he was too nice.

5 James McCudden

James McCudden was born a soldier. His father was a sergeant in the Royal Engineers, his grandfather had been a corporal in the Royal Irish Rangers and there had been Royal Marines in his mother's family for a century. He came into the world in the hospital inside Brompton Barracks, Gillingham, in 1895; among the first sounds he heard were the distant bellowing of drill sergeants and marching feet. Families like the McCuddens were the backbone of an Army which policed the British Empire and they were proud of their military heritage. Boys like James and his three brothers were known as 'barrack rats' and they were moulded from an early age to be the next generation of soldiers. They were nurtured in the bosom of the Army: army houses, army schools with uniformed teachers, army camps as playgrounds, a life of constant awareness of discipline and order.

James's father served in the Royal Engineers for twenty-eight years, starting as a bugler in 1879; he rose to the rank of sergeant major and finished as an instructor at the School of Military Engineering. Even in retirement McCudden senior stayed with the Army; he found a clerical job at Albemarle Fort and when the family moved to Sheerness James went to the garrison school. James's elder brother, William, had enlisted as a bugler in the Royal Engineers before their father retired.

At Eastchurch, near Sheerness, there was a big open space which some early British aviators used for trials and James spent hours hanging around the boundary watching them, fascinated by their exotic machines. It was 1909, the year that Blériot's cross-Channel flight stirred Britain. The excitement of flying stirred in the young McCudden but he would have to wait; when he was fifteen years and one month old, James followed his brother into the Royal Engineers as a bugler and was posted to Gibraltar. His interest in aeroplanes remained and in between his duties as a bugler on The Rock and learning his calling as a boy soldier, he read all the flying magazines he could lay his hands on.

If one boy soldier was hooked on flying, at the time, the British Army was not really sure what to make of aeroplanes. J. T. Moore-Brabazon, one of the intrepid pilots whom James had watched experimenting at Eastchurch, tried to generate some interest at the War Office and he even offered to lend them two machines for their manoeuvres to demonstrate their value; he was turned down. He found that the Army had a curiously 'sporting' attitude towards taking photographs from the air; it seemed that aerial photography was regarded as not really playing the game.

Gradually, though, the Army realised that aircraft might be of some military value. In 1911, the Royal Engineers formed an Air Battalion: No. 1 Company looked after airships, No. 2 Company handled aircraft. It was a small unit, five aeroplanes (one Blériot monoplane and four biplanes), thirty-six horses, fourteen officers and 176 other ranks. It was a highly disciplined unit but both officers and men were for the most part flying enthusiasts so it was a very dedicated one too. One of the 'other ranks' in No. 2 Company was James's brother, Sapper William McCudden.

As foreign powers began forming military air services of one kind and another, the Committee of Imperial Defence reported that the British Army should have one too. Consequently, on 13 May 1912, the Royal Flying Corps was formed. It was a grudging decision and the new Corps was starved of funds and not given a very clear policy, so much of the organisation and the experiment was carried out on the initiative of the officers.

All the original RFC pilots were officers and they had to pay privately for their flying instruction, being reimbursed if they passed their certificate. Views on whether non-commissioned officers should be taught to fly differed: aircraft were seen exclusively as a means of reconnaissance, not as fighting machines. One argument said that NCOs should be trained to fly in the same way as a chauffeur was trained to drive a car, so that the NCO could pilot his officer round the sky to carry out his more important job of observation. But there were officer pilots already and others argued that it would be unfair to expect a soldier to do the same job as an officer with his lower status and pay. As an experiment, some NCOs from 3 Squadron were selected for pilot training and William McCudden was one of them; he became the fourth NCO pilot in the RFC in August 1912.

While William was learning to fly, James was learning more basic soldiering skills in Gibraltar: marching, shooting and how to care for himself, his weapons and his kit. He had not been particularly happy in the Army at first; he was rather a shy boy and he suffered at the hands of some insensitive NCOs. But, away from home, he grew up fast and learned quickly and he became an extremely good shot with a rifle. When he returned to Britain, he applied to join the RFC; he was determined to follow in William's footsteps. His rudimentary aeronautical knowledge stood him in good stead and he was posted to Farnborough in May 1913 as an engine fitter.

Farnborough was literally buzzing with aviation. It was an intoxicating place for a young man like James: a heavy scent of cellulose 'dope', new-mown grass and burnt castor oil blew through the hangars and billets. Above, on the long summer days, pilots took the frail assortment of machines up and puttered round the sky, experimenting with ways to employ them for military purposes. They tried spotting for artillery, they put wireless sets on board, trailing long aerials behind, they mounted machine-guns and cameras on board and developed observation techniques.

It was a paradise for McCudden. When he was off duty, he went to the hangars and sat in the Blériots and Maurice Farman Longhorns, waggling the controls, pretending that he was flying. As an Air Mechanic, one of his first lessons was swinging the propeller to start an engine, a hazardous job unless done properly. One day in the hangar, he decided to practise his pull and to his horror, the engine started and the Caudron rolled forward, chewing its way through part of a Farman and the commanding officer's car. Somebody else had been playing in the cockpit and left the ignition switches on. He was lucky in his CO; his only punishment was seven days' detention.

It was while he was waiting to be sentenced for his 'crime' that a day he had longed for arrived – he made his first flight. One of the pilots, Lieutenant James, must have seen the beam in his eyes, begging for a flight, and so James McCudden made his first flight unofficially in a B. E. 2. Next, he persuaded his brother, by then a fully-fledged pilot, to go one better than Lieutenant James and give him unofficial flying lessons. He had a persuasive tongue and a way of getting what he wanted.

3 Squadron was posted to Netheravon and McCudden was given charge of the engine of a two-seater Blériot flown by Lieutenant Conran. For the pilots and the ground staff, these were days of stimulating hard work but there was, too, a carefree quality about the RFC, an esprit de corps born of being small, new and staffed almost entirely by enthusiasts whatever their job. In the summer of 1914, when they went on manoeuvres, the pilots flew cross-country

while the ground crews went by road and when they met up, the squadron camped with the aircraft, sleeping under the wings.

In August 1914, the European armies faced each other with a dazzling array of new weapons, the fruits of the Industrial Revolution of the previous century. The weapons were new but the thinking behind their use was old: both infantry and cavalry had to contend with massively increased firepower from machine-guns and from artillery, the range of which had grown in a few decades from hundreds of yards to several miles, and the gunners could no longer even see their targets. There was one development which some soldiers didn't even concede was a weapon – the aeroplane. Traditionally, soldiers had gained their strategic intelligence through the use of cavalry and though some senior commanders saw some value in aircraft, most still saw cavalry as the principle means of collecting information. A consequence of that type of thinking was that when the Royal Flying Corps went to France, it was minute, ill-equipped and, by comparison with the air arms of the French and German armies, given a low priority.

McCudden hoped to fly out to France in the two-seater Blériot but at the last moment Lieutenant Conran was given a single-seater Morane Parasol so he had to go by sea. The RFC made its base outside Amiens and when McCudden and the ground party arrived the airfield was bustling with activity. Each aircraft had a ground crew of two: an engine fitter and a rigger, responsible for keeping the maze of wires which braced the fuselage and wings in proper trim. McCudden worked with a rigger called Abrahams and one of their first jobs was to fix wooden racks on the outside of the aircraft to carry grenades. They were to be used offensively as bombs, to be dropped on German soldiers, and defensively against German aircraft. There was already a rack inside for the pilot's rifle.

On 16 August the British Army was preparing for battle; Sir John French was planning an offensive at Mons and 3 Squadron moved to Maubeuge, an airfield nearby. The aircraft went straight into action, probing over the unfamiliar landscape for signs of the Germans. South of the British was the French 5th Army under General Lanzarac. Two officers from 3 Squadron reported that they had seen heavy fighting between the French and the Germans and that the French were retreating, exposing the British flank. Sir John French was sceptical; far from being pleased with such swift reports and acting on them, he continued to plan an offensive.

The Germans sent reconnaissance aircraft over, too, and on 22

August one flew over Maubeuge at about 2000 feet. McCudden turned out with everybody who could handle a gun and they blazed away with rifles and pistols but without effect. Some of the British pilots took off in pursuit but never caught it; it was the first German aircraft McCudden had seen.

Another British reconnaissance flight reported seeing a whole German Corps moving along the Brussels–Ninove road and this time Sir John French could no longer ignore the information he was getting from the air; he called off the offensive. When the Germans attacked, the British regiments were ready and they gave a fierce response but it was only a prelude to retreat.

The German Army swept across northern France and the Allies fell back towards Paris. The retreat from Mons was on; over the next ten days, McCudden and 3 Squadron operated from nine different airfields in ten days.

It was a time of nonstop work for men and aircraft. Engines 'coked up' frequently on the long flights and McCudden spent most nights grinding valves ready for the morning. At first light, the aircraft would fly their missions and meet up with the ground party later in the day. Thanks to McCudden's work, the Parasol's engine barely skipped a beat and he began flying from airfield to airfield in one of the two-seaters, ready to start work as soon as he landed. Pilots and ground crews learnt a lot in those few days and they learnt it while fending for themselves and living through the demoralising shambles of headlong retreat. They lived rough: meals, when they got them, were cooked over a petrol tin and supplemented with apples scrumped from orchards by the road, Lieutenant Conran milked a cow, McCudden had his first bath since leaving England in the ornamental pool of an abandoned convent. There was no complaint; the 'old army', as it became known later after the influx of thousands of conscripts, was made up of men who, like McCudden, could keep going under extreme pressure and fatigue and when the time came, turn and fight.

The retreat stopped before Paris and French and British aircraft were kept busy supplying details of German movements to generals thirsty for information gleaned from the air. The tide turned at the Battle of the Marne, a battle planned largely on the basis of aerial reconnaissance. The Allies pushed the Germans back and by mid-September they faced each other from trenches across the static lines which were to be the dominant feature of that war.

3 Squadron operated from airfields about fifteen to twenty miles behind the Front and from landing-grounds much nearer. They

often had to make their airfields from scratch. Once they made one out of a beetfield by borrowing a roller and getting some Indian cavalry to tow it up and down to form a runway; then the whole squadron turned out and marched up and down to harden the surface. The observers spotted for the guns in the big artillery duels which followed and their pilots developed techniques of aerial photography, building up maps of the lines.

Autumn came and the weather changed but work went on; McCudden worked in the open on cold, wet nights, stripping the Parasol's engine and reassembling it with all the fiddly little nuts and bolts. Improvisation and experiment went on, too, sometimes with tragic consequences; once the squadron experimented with Melanite bombs but while they were rigging up a release system two bombs exploded, killing eleven men.

Through the winter and into spring it went on: artillery spotting, photographing the changing pattern of the lines, grinding valves, stripping engines and improvising. McCudden worked hard and his results were consistently good; in April 1915 he reached the rank of sergeant and was put in charge of all the engines on a flight, rising from air mechanic to sergeant in less than a year. A month later his brother William was killed in a flying accident in Britain. Undaunted, if not even more determined to fly, he applied for pilot training. He was turned down; at least, his application was deferred because of his value as a mechanic.

In November, the squadron got a new CO, Major Ludlow-Hewitt, and it was he who gave McCudden his first chance to fly operationally as an observer. Being the least experienced man, the CO took McCudden. Observers did not have logbooks at that time so McCudden recorded his flights in an old school exercise book, including his first combat in an aeroplane on 19 December 1915.

He was with Lieutenant Saunders in a Morane. They were the last in a line of three aircraft sent to look at the railway marshalling yards at Valenciennes. On the way they had to fly close to the German airfield at Douai. By this time, both sides had started to counter the threat from reconnaissance aircraft by using fast single-seaters whose sole function was to shoot them down. On this flight they were attacked by a Fokker Monoplane 'scout' with a synchronised machine-gun firing through the propeller, Germany's most deadly aircraft of the time.

Faster than the Moranes, the Fokkers could attack from behind in a shallow dive. The German pilot went for the middle aircraft in the flight, then turned in front and attacked Saunders and

McCudden head on. There was no gun-mounting to fire forwards, so McCudden stood up in the cockpit with the Lewis gun to his shoulder and fired as the Fokker passed over the right wing and disappeared behind them. He scanned all around. Far below he could see more German aircraft taking off from Douai, then he saw the Fokker again, this time climbing up from under their tail. He shouted to Saunders to turn, to give him a better field of fire, then waited until the enemy was about three hundred yards away and fired a burst. The German pilot turned quickly, climbed and dived at them again. McCudden let him come to three hundred yards, then fired. This time the German retired to a safe distance and stayed there. They flew over the railyards at Valenciennes and counted the rolling stock, then headed back to the Allied lines. Over Douai again, the Fokker flew away, but the aircraft which McCudden had seen taking off earlier were the slower two-seaters and could not reach the British aircraft in time. McCudden fired a few bursts in their direction to keep them at bay.

They were all convinced that the pilot of the Fokker had been Immelmann. Immelmann was a legend and the Germans, like the French, publicised their 'aces'. The British Army felt that the practice was invidious. Invidious or not, in the case of Immelmann, the publicity had an effect on Allied pilots' morale; so great was his reputation that an encounter with him was felt to be certain death. Back on the ground, McCudden was elated; he had survived combat with Immelmann and when he deliberated on the fight he realised that even the great Immelmann was not invincible against the right defensive tactics. McCudden's tactical sense and coolness under fire had been noted; once the CO had congratulated them all, he asked McCudden to fly with him the same afternoon. They ran into another Fokker and McCudden used the same tactics – anticipation, a sharp look-out and short accurate bursts whenever the enemy came within range. Ludlow-Hewitt performed some violent manoeuvres to throw the German off, but McCudden urged his CO to fly straight and level, to attract the German whom he passionately wanted to shoot down, but the German flew away.

McCudden often flew with Ludlow-Hewitt after that. He was very keen to learn to fly and he knew that the CO could help him. As a professional soldier he knew, too, that in war there were opportunities to advance his career much faster than in peacetime. He flew with the major on Christmas Day and Boxing Day and on into January, demonstrating his skill as a marksman and as a tactician and his aggressiveness as a soldier. His ebullience, his stories and his relationship with the CO did not go unnoticed in the Sergeants' Mess; his messmates saw the self-confidence it brought as naked ambition tarred with conceit. In a letter to his mother, he told her how jealous they were and he almost seemed to relish their gibes and their sarcasm because, underneath, he knew precisely what he was doing.

In January 1916 he got his reward; he was promoted to flight sergeant, awarded the Croix de Guerre by General Joffre and posted home to Britain to begin training as a pilot.

After two weeks' leave he began flying lessons at Farnborough. There were only two training aircraft there at the time and both had been crashed by other students so his career as a pilot got off to a slow start. Then in April, he was posted to Gosport and things began to happen much more quickly. After just four hours of dual instruction, he made his first solo flight and qualified for his Aero Club certificate the same day by flying a figure-of-eight and landing within fifty yards of a designated spot. By early May, he was an assistant instructor himself; by the end of the month he was regraded a First Class Flyer; in July he was posted to No. 20 Squadron back in France. The speed with which he mastered flying was partly due to his own enthusiasm but it was also the result of the 'unofficial' flying lessons with his brother and others; and having flown as an observer in combat he was completely at home in an aeroplane, even when it was being thrown violently around the sky.

20 Squadron flew the F.E.2d, a two-seater with a powerful Rolls-Royce engine and a 'pusher' propeller at the back. The pilot sat just in front of the engine and the gunner/observer sat right in the nose. McCudden flew his first operations as a pilot in the F.E.2d but with his aggressiveness and marksmanship, he was a natural choice to fly fighters and before long he was posted to fly the single-seat D.H.2 with No. 29 Squadron. The RFC needed aggressive pilots because they were pursuing an aggressive policy, carrying the fight over the German lines. He found some familiar faces there: the CO was Major Conran with whom he had gone to war two years before and he had taught one of the pilots, Lieutenant Bowman, to fly.

The D.H.2 was a real fighting aeroplane, one of Britain's answers to the scurge of the Fokkers, and McCudden had his first combat victory in one. He was patrolling between Armentières and Ypres on 6 September 1916 at 14,000 feet. He saw a two-seater near Gheluwe, but the German turned east, diving towards his own lines. McCudden went into a screaming dive and gave chase, but when he got to within four hundred yards he stopped gaining. Unable to get closer, McCudden fired a whole drum from the Lewis gun just for luck. There was no effect and they both continued to dive as McCudden changed the drum of ammunition. He fired again before the German disappeared into a cloud. In his combat report, he simply reported the chase, making no claim, but three days later he heard that it crashed near the Menin Road. A month later he was awarded the Military Medal.

That autumn he patrolled the Western Front daily and fought many inconclusive battles. His combat reports were detailed and accurate and they attracted attention further up the command structure. The professional soldier shone through: he was disciplined and cool in a fight, his actions came from training and experience rather than emotion, and he could control his natural aggression until it was needed. His technical knowledge was greater than almost all the officers on the Squadron and he had an understanding of air fighting which was the equal of most of them. He never questioned the system which kept him apart from the officers, though most of them were doing exactly the same job as he was, but his ambitious streak was always pushing him on and, in November 1916, he applied for a commission.

The same month, McCudden took part in a classic air battle. The fighter squadrons of both sides fought each other for air superiority, control of the skies, so that the reconnaissance aircraft could work more safely. He was on an offensive patrol across the lines with five others, looking for a fight; three turned back with engine trouble leaving McCudden, Noakes, a fellow NCO pilot, and Lieutenant Ball. Noakes was the most experienced, so he took the lead. They ran into a patrol of five German Albatros fighters on the German side of the lines. The D.H.2 was more manoeuvrable but the Albatros was faster and with their superior numbers the Germans had a tactical advantage. One German dived and attacked them in front, turning at the last moment, inviting McCudden to follow. He did, and within seconds he felt a sickening shudder and heard the sound of ripping fabric as a second Albatros hit him from behind. Noakes was getting the same treatment. Fleetingly, McCudden saw Ball flying straight and level while changing a drum of ammunition. One of the Germans was on his tail. The fight lasted twenty minutes and it was all close combat, twisting and turning at the last second to evade the enemy, getting in a squirt of fire as an opportunity arose. The three British pilots gave each other what protection they could and gradually the fight moved west towards their home lines where the

Germans broke off. All three D.H.2s were badly damaged and they had to be flown gingerly back to base. The CO had had a running commentary on the fight over the telephone from a British anti-aircraft battery and he was there to greet them. On the ground, they found further evidence of the fierceness and closeness of the battle: McCudden's aircraft was spattered with blood from one of the German pilots.

No claims were made but it was the kind of dogfight around which the legend of World War One fighter pilots was made: individual, chivalrous combat high in the sky, golden morning sun glinting off tumbling wings and spinning propellers, chattering machine-guns and bellowing engines. From the mud and the limb-strewn trenches below, where thousands of soldiers gazed up at these epics, it may have had a chivalrous quality but in the air no quarter was asked or given. It was a case of getting in close behind the enemy quickly, and shooting him in the back if possible.

Recounting battles like that in the Sergeants' Mess, with all the exuberance of youth and satisfaction of success, McCudden was accused by some non-flying men of line-shooting; they thought him arrogant and conceited. Perhaps he was, but to fight like that sometimes twice daily, then return to base with the aircraft shot up, possibly having seen a friend killed, and then prepare to go back at a moment's notice again and again, he needed constantly to reinforce his spirits and talking about it helped to build confidence. Confidence was not even enough, he had to be invincible. Most of the pilots were officers and in their separate Mess, they were able to talk their battles through with each other.

To be a successful fighter pilot and survive, he needed to cultivate his natural aggression and good marksmanship to press home an attack at close range. His senses had to be tuned to anticipate every possible manoeuvre by the enemy, his head had to be kept clear while adrenalin pumped through the body. McCudden was an excellent pilot but superb flying did not win battles, frequently a fighter pilot had to be brutal with his aircraft, changing direction as violently as the structure of the aircraft would allow. McCudden understood his aircraft, how it flew, how to get the best out of its engine and armament. Like most British pilots, he was plagued by jamming guns and he spent hours on the ground carefully selecting each bullet himself, loading his own guns and testing them frequently.

Each fight taught him something new about German tactics and increased his own experience so that next time he would be able to anticipate the enemy a little bit earlier, get into a slightly better firing position. In analysing combat a pilot could not afford judgements born of excitement and exaggeration. James McCudden was a professional; he had an analytical mind and an ability to make detailed observations of enemy aircraft and tactics in the heat of a fight. He had a professional regard for the enemy and frequently recorded good flying by his opponents in his combat reports. But he remained coolly detached when it came to killing them.

In December 1916, he heard that he had been given a commission. He went home on leave and returned to 29 Squadron in the uniform of a second lieutenant. His score was still only one and he was anxious to improve it so he went looking for fights. At that time the Germans had the upper hand as they had generally superior aircraft, but McCudden began to score despite the advantage.

On 15 February his score had risen to four and he was leading a patrol near Adinfer Wood when he saw two German Roland aircraft flying low. He signalled to the flight and dived towards the enemy but he outdived the rest and was alone when he attacked. He fired at the leading machine and was promptly attacked by the other. McCudden was a man of unfailing personal courage but he knew when to break off a fight and when to continue and when he came under attack he left the fight and rejoined his patrol. Shortly afterwards, he saw the same Roland flying back across British territory and he dived to attack again. He opened fire and tangled with the German, fighting him down to just three hundred feet above the trenches where he managed to get into a good position at fifty yards. He could see the German gunner clinging to the side of the fuselage with one arm while erratically firing a machine-gun at him with the other; he may have been wounded. McCudden put on a new drum of ammunition and emptied it into the aircraft at very close range. The enemy pilot tried to make a forced landing but the Roland broke up on the ground. It was McCudden's fifth victory.

When he landed after that flight the CO described him as a 'young tiger'. He was delighted; once again, McCudden's aggression and skill had not gone unnoticed and he was recommended for the Military Cross which was approved the next day.

McCudden had been fighting for eight months and was just getting into his stride as an operational fighter pilot when he was posted back to England. The RFC was expanding rapidly and with his knowledge and experience he was more use as an instructor.

His heart was really back in France where the fighting was and in June 1917, he went back on a 'refresher course', to do some fighting so that he could improve on his instructing. He was sent to 66 Squadron and flew on patrols but the visit was notable not so much for that but because, while he was there, 56 Squadron invited him to dinner. 56 Squadron was an élite unit and its pilots were already a legend in the RFC: they flew the latest S.E.5 fighter; Captain Albert Ball, Britain's 'ace of aces', had been one of the flight commanders until his death in May; and they had a reputation for high scoring in the air and good living on the ground. The CO, Major Blomfield, invited McCudden to go on a patrol with the squadron and he eagerly accepted. It was his first ever flight in an S.E.5. He flew straight into combat but shot nothing down. In the battle, however, he once again displayed all his fighting qualities and clearly impressed the CO. He was desperate to join 56 and told the CO precisely what he wanted.

He went back to England, but only briefly. In August he was not only posted to 56 Squadron, but, now promoted to captain, he was to be one of the three flight commanders. It was a great moment for him; being able to call himself a flight commander on 56 Squadron gave him the greatest pleasure.

One of the other flight commanders was his old pupil Bowman, the other Captain Maxwell. The CO did not do much operational flying, his task was to organise the squadron in such a way as to leave the flight commanders free to concentrate on training the pilots and fighting. That was what Blomfield wanted McCudden for – the pushiness and leadership which McCudden clearly possessed – and though in this more enlightened age it seems strange to have to record it, he was far-sighted enough to put aside the social gulf between the ex-ranker and most of the pilots in the squadron to get him.

The night McCudden joined them they dined formally in the Mess. He and Bowman sat either side of the CO and he looked down the splendid tables at the other pilots. They were a picked bunch. In McCudden's flight there was Arthur Rhys-Davids, former Captain of Eton, winner of a Balliol scholarship, with eleven Germans to his credit; there was Lieutenant Barlow, a trained engineer. There was Richard Mayberry, late of the cavalry, Sandhurst and Wellington; there were musicians, an architect and career officers. McCudden felt the differences acutely and in conversations other than about fighting and flying he was out of his depth. At times like that he wished fervently that he had had a public-school education.

The next morning he inspected 'B' flight and demonstrated his technical knowledge to the ground staff who were more used to dealing with pilots who hardly ever looked under the cowlings. He had his S.E.5 tuned just the way he wanted and then led his team out on patrol.

Within days of arriving at 56 he started scoring: 18 August, an Albatros D down near Houthem; 19 August, another at Gheluvelt; 20 August, two more near Polygon Wood. The Albatros D was no easy target, it was one of Germany's foremost fighters at the time.

One of those kills was McCudden's first 'flamerino'. He and his flight had managed to take a whole flight of Germans by surprise and when they dived to attack, McCudden went for their leader, firing both guns from 150 yards right up to fifty. He raked the German and saw spurts of fire. The dope-covered fabric, wood and fuel caught quickly and the fire rapidly grew into an inferno which engulfed the machine as it spiralled down. At fifty yards he could see the man in the cockpit and the sight of such a death at close quarters touched even the highly professional and unemotional McCudden. He was not a man of great imagination but it took very little to realise what was happening to the German pilot. He felt sick but as he said: 'I had to live down my better feelings.'

His personal score and his flight's mounted. In another fight, they came up against a very skilled German pilot in one of the new Fokker Triplanes, a highly manoeuvrable machine with a very good rate of climb, though slightly slower than the S.E.5. McCudden and his team came upon him as he was attacking a lone S.E.5 of 60 Squadron. The German was either recklessly brave or over-confident of his own skill and performance for he decided to fight it out. He pulled every stunt in his repertoire, twisting and turning and climbing, trying to get on a British tail, a magnificent fighter as McCudden later acknowledged. At one point McCudden saw him at the apex of a cone of fire from all five of his flight's guns but still he fought on. But the odds were severely against him and when he started the fight he could not have known who he was up against. Finally, Rhys-Davids got behind him with a long and accurate burst and McCudden saw him fall. Next day they found out that the pilot had been Werner Voss, one of Germany's most celebrated aces who had shot down 48 Allied aircraft.

That autumn McCudden was awarded a bar to his Military Cross and the Distinguished Service Order. The DSO was for his leadership and that was what he was there for. He had made his pilots into a fighting team and he constantly drilled them on technique: never take unnecessary risks, get in close before firing, concentrate on accurate shooting, beware of traps set by the enemy. The tally of his flight while he was in command is revealing: while he was with 56, the squadron shot down 175 enemy aircraft for the loss of 21; 'B' flight's share was 77 of which McCudden accounted for 52 and he lost only four pilots.

There were rumblings within the RFC that McCudden always went out for himself and certainly towards the end of his time with 56 he became obsessional about shooting down more enemy. He wanted to score, because that was what he was there for and because he was highly ambitious. But the evidence of his combat reports shows that he was not given either to exaggeration or false claims; indeed they give the opposite impression and he was always at pains to give credit for good flying and fighting even if it was by the enemy.

December 1917 was bitterly cold on the Western Front. The thermometer outside the pilot's hut at Elstree Blanche showed 20 degrees below freezing and the airfield was white with frost. Underfoot, bare, frozen earth showed where the summer grass had been worn by the constant coming and going of aircraft. The morning was still and the sounds of barked orders and the clang of heavy tools carried far on the chill air. Occasionally the far distant rumble of artillery carried across the barren countryside and through the leafless trees. McCudden, swathed in layer upon layer of clothing, waddled out to his S.E.5 and eased himself into the cockpit. His patrol was classified as a special; he was going alone.

'Switches off?' called the mechanic, who was standing by the propeller.

'Switches off,' confirmed the pilot.

'Sucking in.'

'Sucking in.'

The mechanic took a propeller blade and eased it round slowly to suck fuel into the cold engine, then stood back.

'Contact!' he shouted to the pilot.

The pilot turned the switches with heavily-gloved hands and responded: 'Contact.'

The mechanic heaved down expertly on the propeller and the engine erupted into life, a burst of oily smoke followed by the healthy roar of 200 horsepower bellowing through the unsilenced exhaust just outside the cockpit. Looking down inside, McCudden checked round the instruments then waved away the chocks. He eased forward, then taxied to the runway, opened the engine to full power, briefly smothering the stillness of the airfield.

Climbing through the clear sky, line after line of trenches

unfolded, zigzagging north and south through the churned-up landscape and over the ever-widening horizon; now and then the blue-black puff of artillery fire stained the scene. But McCudden had little time for the view, he looked for the familiar landmarks, the shape of the woods and the lie of roads and railways. And all the time his head was moving, eyes searching for the first sign of an enemy aircraft.

At 17,500 feet the air was much colder than on the ground: his hands, feet and nose were numbed and the cold slowly seeped through his clothing; goggles frosted and stuck to an ungreased part of his face; there was less oxygen, so breathing increased and the cold air chilled him from the inside. The air was thinner and his blood pressure rose until the space between his brain and his skull all but disappeared and a tight feeling gripped his scalp. And all the time his head kept moving, eyes darting, searching the sky, especially near the glare of the sun, for a sign of the enemy.

He had taken off at 10.15 a.m. and just after 11.00 he saw one coming west over Boursies: a Rumpler reconnaissance machine. The German didn't spot him. McCudden slid the S.E.5 into an enemy blind spot and closed fast. At seventy-five yards he fired a short burst then looked up. Almost immediately the enemy aircraft keeled over and the right-hand wing fell off. McCudden had hit a vital part of the structure. It spiralled down and crashed just north of Vélu Wood. Fifteen minutes later he found another flying north above Haplincourt. He went through the same procedure; this time the enemy aircraft caught fire and tumbled down, trailing charred shreds of burnt fabric. Shortly afterwards, he sent another down in flames, then attacked a fourth but he had to leave that one still under control at 9000 feet, gliding towards the German lines; he was low on petrol after two hours and had to return to base.

Early in 1918 he was awarded a bar to his DSO. The time had come for him to go back to England for another tour as an instructor. He was famous within the RFC and when they 'dined him out' it was with style. All the squadrons in the Brigade, and the local French commandant, came to see him off and the speeches embarrassed him. The next day he dined with the brigade commander, General Higgins, and the day after that with the commander of the Third Army, General Sir Julian Byng.

On 1 April 1918, the RFC was disbanded and the Royal Air Force was formed. The next day McCudden was awarded the Victoria Cross. He was a national hero now, of the type the Germans had in Richthofen. Gillingham prepared to make him a

Freeman, he began to write his autobiography with the help of Mrs Alec-Tweedie and the Editor of *The Aeroplane*, C. G. Grey. On 6 April he went to Buckingham Palace to receive his VC, DSO and MC from the King. He had come a long way in the six years since he had played the bugle in Gibraltar.

There were really only two more achievements he could aim for in the immediate future: to shoot down more aircraft than anybody else, including the German ace Richthofen, and to command a squadron. Both were achievable only in France. He could have stayed in Britain as an instructor or a staff officer and even though his younger brother Anthony had been killed in aerial combat earlier that year, it made no difference, he wanted to go back and he usually got what he wanted.

A sour note was sounded when it was suggested that he command 85 Squadron. According to the diary of an American pilot on the squadron, the rumour that he only went out for himself stood against him and the pilots expressed a collective wish to their general not to have him as their commander. Less creditably, he also recorded that the British element in the squadron objected because he had been a 'Tommy' and his father a sergeant major in the 'old army'. Whatever the reason, he did not go to 85, but by a wry twist of fate, it went to 'Mick' Mannock whose father had been a corporal.

He was promoted to major and given command of 60 Squadron, and set out to take over his new command in a brand-new S.E.5 on 9 July. On the way he landed at an airfield close to his destination to ask the way. He took off again and crashed into a wood on the aircraft boundary; he died later that evening.

The reason for the crash was never established and there has been a slight air of mystery about McCudden's death ever since. He was a superb pilot and a war hero and the possibility that it could have been simple pilot error or a mechanical failure seemed too improbable at the time. Curiously, he was not strapped in when he crashed.

His death was a great loss to the newly-formed RAF. He was a popular hero and there was still plenty of fighting to be done in the air. Important though his personal aggression and individual skill would have been, it was in the development of tactics and leadership in the air that he made his greatest contribution. He had seen the whole of the development of aerial tactics and seen it at first-hand.

War and the profession of arms consumed his whole life and he matured from a boy into a man in the hectic but narrow world of an army at war. His skills, apart from his flying ability, were those of unique importance in war, particularly the new and menacing war in the air: personal courage, controlled aggression, a trained, unemotional response to dangerous situations, an acute tactical sense and an ability to appreciate very quickly how to fight a particular battle. Despite its horrors, the war in France was a powerful magnet for him. It was his element, it was where he could express his full potential and use his undoubted abilities. He had that acute awareness which was vital to survival in the air war, the uncanny ability to see the enemy first, anticipate his movements and use the vital few seconds to good advantage.

Skills invaluable in war but of limited application in peace. He was a regular soldier and would no doubt have been able to stay on in the RAF after the war, but he had risen with the massive tide of expansion in military aviation and would have had to contend with the equally massive decline which followed. His rise in rank was equally astounding – from air mechanic to bemedalled major in five years – and in the post-war years there would have been less of an outlet for his ambitious streak.

James McCudden was a soldier, a soldier's soldier. Today, he is best remembered within the fighter pilot fraternity, especially in No. 56 Squadron RAF where the fighting spirit and aggressive traditions he helped to establish remain central to its ethos and its effectiveness.

6 Manfred von Richthofen

In May 1917, Rittmeister Manfred Freiherr von Richthofen, the 'Red Baron', was at the zenith of his popularity and the peak of his fighting career: 52 aerial victories, 21 of them in the previous month alone – 'Bloody April' as it became known to the Royal Flying Corps.

In the Army and throughout the German nation, among Germany's allies and its enemies, the name Richthofen evoked powerful emotions: a love of the fatherland, the supremacy of the German Army and the virtues and heroism of its officer class. Ordinary people scanned their newspapers daily for stories of his victories in the air; his photograph was worshipped by countless schoolgirls and his deeds were the dreams of countless schoolboys. Everywhere he went, officers, soldiers and civilians gathered; the high- and low-born paid him tribute.

That May he went to Kreuznach, the German Supreme Headquarters, where he had interviews with Germany's two highest-ranking commanders, von Hindenburg and Ludendorff, then he dined with the Emperor, Wilhelm II. It was his birthday and the Kaiser presented him with a gift and they chatted through the meal; the 'all-high war-lord' basking in the younger man's glory.

The lionising didn't end at Kreuznach: the next day he went to Bad Homburg for lunch with the Empress Victoria and another little birthday gift. Then on to Berlin and finally to the family home, Schweidnitz, in Silesia, for some leave and some hunting on the family estates.

Manfred von Richthofen's tall, lean body bore all the hallmarks of the Prussian aristocracy. His finely-proportioned features testified to centuries of breeding, his body language exuded effortless self-confidence and his presence was that of one who leads and commands.

In the late eighteenth century his ancestors supported Frederick the Great against the Austrian Emperor, and the family title,

Freiherr (Baron), was the reward for service to the German Emperors. His family had held land, power and influence in Silesia, in East Prussia, even before the time of Frederick the Great and the Richthofens had prospered for centuries as clergymen, eminent judges and lawyers.

His own father had been a soldier but he had left the Army because of bad health. Manfred was his eldest son; he was born in 1892 and his early upbringing was perfect for a young boy of rude good health and boundless energy. The family home at Schweidnitz had acres of countryside to wander in, trees to climb, rivers to swim in, horses to ride and game to shoot. The estates of his extended family were open to him for holidays and he made good use of them to indulge his passion for hunting.

This carefree existence came to an abrupt end in 1903 when he entered the military school at Wahlstatt at the age of eleven. It was a hard life for a young boy: the task of the Prussian military schools was to provide officers for the Imperial Army, an army with a tradition of the strictest possible discipline and a reputation for thoroughness which was well deserved. The function of the curriculum was to steep the cadets in the values of obedience, self-discipline, love of the fatherland and service to the Emperor and it achieved its ends by means of a rigorous timetable of study, highly competitive sports and spartan living conditions. Manfred was high-spirited and individualistic and he detested the school but he saw it as a hurdle which he would have to overcome and stuck it out, doing just enough to get through and stay out of trouble. Occasionally he had to find an outlet for his exuberance and on one occasion, he climbed the steeple of Wahlstatt church and tied his handkerchief to the top.

In the spring of 1911 he went into the army proper. He had put his name down to join the 1st (Kaiser Alexander III's) Uhlans, a cavalry regiment in which many of his relatives served; he was delighted when they accepted him. The regiment was stationed in the garrison town of Ostrovo, close to the Russian border, but more importantly for young Manfred, it was close to his home in Silesia. In 1912, after nine years of military education, he was promoted to Leutnant and he was very proud to hear himself addressed as 'Herr Leutnant'.

Life in the German Imperial Army was strict, but life with the regiment had abundant pleasures for a young officer like Manfred: there were plenty of opportunities for sport, especially riding, and the family estates were close by, where he could continue to enjoy hunting.

Above: Orville Wright. Below: Wilbur Wright

Louis Blériot

Above: A. V. Roe. Below: Samuel F. Cody

James McCudden

Manfred von Richthofen

Charles Lindbergh

Charles Yeager

John Young

Germany and Russia had fought over the plains of East Prussia for centuries. In 1914, Germany had to fight on two fronts but her military planners had decided to make the thrust in the west first, against France, and after that to turn its attention to its more traditional enemy in the east. Manfred was right on the border, on the Eastern Front, and his first job in the war was to gather intelligence about Russian strength and movements. He rode over the border with six soldiers who then carried his despatches back to base. They went to the village of Kieltze, just inside Russia, where he placed one of his men in the church tower as a look-out. To ensure the compliant behaviour of the local population, he locked the local Orthodox priest in his own church and assured him, and the villagers, that if they misbehaved by giving away the presence of his unit, the priest would be killed. It was crude but effective and he stayed in the village undetected for five days, sending regular reports back to his headquarters. On the fifth night, the observer in the church tower reported that Cossacks were approaching. Richthofen stole through the churchyard to take a closer look at the enemy and counted about thirty men. Too many for a fight. He took his few remaining men, roamed a little further looking for Russian troops and then returned to base.

After a few weeks on the Eastern Front the Uhlans were shipped across Germany to join in the offensive against France. Richthofen observed in a letter to his parents that a soldier becomes rapidly accustomed to crudeness in wartime: he slept rough, he did not wash or change his clothes and the only way to get sufficient food was to threaten violence. The crudeness of war did no appear to worry him; he noted, almost laconically, that when some Belgians 'had rebelled against our cavalry . . . it had been necessary to line a number of them up against the wall!'

The German military machine was in a ruthless and determined mood; the plan was to advance quickly into France, heading for Paris. The Uhlans were soon in action: Richthofen was ordered to take a small force to reconnoitre a forest near Virton and assess the strength of the French – a difficult task in a thick forest. As they rode along the paths, looking for signs of the enemy, the patrol came under musket-fire from the window of a forester's cottage, wounding one of his men and a horse. Richthofen had the house surrounded immediately, then he went inside where he found several boys. He was blazing with anger and threatened to shoot them all if they did not hand over the guilty one; they made a dash for it, he fired after them but missed. Having found the muskets, he took his revenge by burning the cottage down.

He resumed the patrol and found fresh tracks. He followed them through the forest and rode straight into a trap. His leading men came up against a barricade across the path; on the right was a high wall, on the left, barbed wire. As soon as his patrol was at a standstill, the French dragoons he had been following opened fire, killing or capturing most of them and scattering the rest in confusion; Richthofen escaped.

The start of the war was an exciting time for a young officer; it was an opportunity to put years of training into practice. Autumn 1914 did have a certain glorious quality before the fighting settled down to the stalemate of the first winter in the trenches, but it became apparent fairly soon that there was little for cavalry to do: reconnaissance on horseback was a nonsense over a muddy, static battlefield covered in barbed wire.

The job he had done on horseback, reconnaissance, was largely in the process of being taken over by aircraft and Richthofen served for a time in the trenches as an infantryman and later as a staff officer. Daily he saw aircraft flying overhead, setting out on intelligence-gathering missions: they looked frail but heroic and exciting. More importantly, they were doing something useful. Richthofen was a man of action and he wanted a chance to do something glorious for his country. He had never flown in an aeroplane but he was a trained military observer and it seemed natural to apply to join the Air Service. In the German Air Service, the observer was usually an officer and the pilot was a non-commissioned officer acting more or less as a chauffeur. He was accepted and by the summer of 1915 he had been trained and was posted once again to the Russian Front.

The German commander in the east, von Mackensen, was driving the Russians back towards Brest-Litovsk and as they retreated, the Russians were scorching the earth behind them. Richthofen teamed up with Erich, Graf von Holck, another young aristocrat, and a pilot who had found flying to his taste, and together they searched the burning countryside. Once they were flying near Wisznice, trying to determine the strength of the Russian columns in the area. There was a huge pall of smoke above the city and all that Richthofen could make out were the fires. As they turned back towards the German lines the engine began to falter. They came lower and lower and soon Richthofen could see Russian soldiers marching along the roads. When they saw the German aircraft within range, they opened fire with machine-guns. The engine was hit and it stopped altogether. Powerless, they glided towards the German lines but ran out of height too soon and had to land near a fortified artillery position which Richthofen had reported only the night before as held by the Russians. On the ground they jumped out quickly and headed for the edge of a nearby forest. They made it to the trees and Richthofen drew his revolver. They prepared to defend themselves. On the far side of the field they saw soldiers approaching their aircraft. Richthofen peered through his field glasses and saw that they wore caps rather than the distinctive German spiked helmet. They feared the worst. In fact they were Prussian grenadiers who had stormed the position that morning.

In August 1915, Richthofen went back to the Western Front to fly in a large aircraft known rather grandly as the *Grosskampfflugzeug* (Great Battle Aeroplane). It was equipped with a machine-gun and it was in one of these monsters that he took part in his first aerial combat. It was against a frail-looking British Farman. As soon as he saw it, Richthofen felt a surge of excitement; he was a huntsman and a crack shot and he was eager to try out the machine-gun in anger. His pilot – Zeumer – moved closer and Richthofen fired a short burst at it. Unlike a game bird, the British pilot reacted swiftly by manoeuvring behind them and firing everything he had. For a time, the two circled round each other, vying for a good firing position, but finally the British pilot broke off the fight. Richthofen blamed Zeumer for not putting him in a good firing position and Zeumer blamed Richthofen for not shooting straight. Richthofen was deeply frustrated that he had not shot it down; he had rather imagined that a few shots would do it. Communication between pilot and observer was difficult at the best of times but in the heat of the battle, in a cumbersome machine, it was hopeless. But from those who survived such encounters and learned from them, successful tactics were born.

Aerial reconnaissance proved a valuable source of intelligence and as the threat it posed to both sides grew, so both sides developed new aircraft and tactics to shoot them down. The Germans were the first to come up with an aircraft specially equipped for this new role, the Fokker Eindecker. It was a single-seat monoplane with a fixed, forward-facing machine-gun which fired through the propeller arc using an ingenious interrupter gear. The pilot was in control of the aircraft, he fired the guns himself and the machine was highly manoeuvrable. The pilots who flew this new breed of aircraft, and who consequently shot down most of the enemy, became the élite of the Air Service. Their job was tailor-made for heroes: fighter pilots combined the traditional qualities of ancient warriors, personal courage, individual fighting skill and esprit, with the mastery of the latest technical developments in modern weapons. For a time, these aircraft, in the right hands, gave Germany a period of ascendancy in the air.

Richthofen was a natural as a fighter pilot. He had a finely developed sense of duty, he was indifferent to personal danger and death and he had a strong desire to personally inflict as much damage on the enemy as possible. Moreover he saw the thrill of the chase, the hunt, in the work of the fighter pilot. Travelling in a railway dining-car one day he met Oswald Boelcke whose reputation as a fighter pilot was second to none. Round his neck he wore the coveted 'Pour le Mérite' medal, the mark of an ace. It was not long after this meeting that Richthofen decided to try to emulate him.

There was an instructional machine at Rethel where Richthofen and Zeumer were based and Zeumer gave him his first flying lessons. At first Richthofen was not a very promising pupil: he took twenty-five hours of instruction before he was ready to go solo and when he did it was a disaster. His attitude owed rather too much to the hero and not enough to the technician. He approached his first landing in a cavalier style; he shut off the engine, turned over the usual tree, just as he had been trained, and waited to see what happened next.

What happened was that the aircraft tipped on its nose and was smashed. Two days later he managed to land in one piece, then he took the flying test, but failed it. Back in Germany, after further training, he took his final test on Christmas Day and passed.

He was not posted to fly fighters at first; he started as the pilot of a two-seater, and in March 1916 he was posted to a squadron stationed near Verdun. His first chance for combat as a pilot came on 26 April 1916. He met up with a French Nieuport over Fort Douaumont but it promptly turned and flew away. He chased it, closed with it, aimed and fired a short burst. The Nieuport rolled over and began to dive and, to start with, both he and his observer thought that the pilot was staging some kind of trick to evade further combat. When it crashed just behind Fort Douaumont, he realised he had shot it down. At that stage of the war, aircraft shot down on the Allied side of the lines did not count towards a pilot's personal score, but he did at least have the satisfaction of reading about it in the Army Report for the day.

A few days later, on a very windy day, he was flying in his two-seater when he saw a Fokker being attacked by three French Caudrons; he turned towards the fight to help the Fokker, but he was downwind of it and could not make any headway and could only watch as the number of Caudrons rose to ten. The Fokker eventually dived into some cloud and at first Richthofen thought it had escaped, but the pilot had been shot straight through the head and it crashed. Later he discovered that the German pilot was his old friend Holck. In a letter home to his parents he described the death of his friend in heroic fashion, a fine death, tumbling down from 10,000 feet with a shot through the head.

Not long afterwards, Richthofen got his chance to fly a Fokker, though he had to share it with another pilot, Reimann. Richthofen flew it in the mornings and Reimann in the afternoons. One afternoon, Reimann was shot down over no-man's-land and though he managed to escape back to the German lines, the aircraft was destroyed.

Richthofen's ambitions to become a fighter pilot were further frustrated when he was once again sent to the Russian Front, this time to fly even heavier aircraft which were being used to bomb railway stations and bridges. While he was away, events in the development of the air war reached a new intensity.

In July 1916 the British mounted an enormous offensive on the Somme. They gained little ground for the huge effort involved, but the German Army was severely battered. In the air, the RFC mounted an offensive too; it adopted a very aggressive policy, flying into German-held airspace, taking the battle to the German Air Service.

The battle was fierce and the losses on both sides were huge – 800 for the RFC and 350 German. To meet this onslaught the German Air Service was completely reorganised. First of all it was separated to some extent from the Army and given its own command structure under the control of air-minded men like General Hoeppner. Hitherto, the Fokkers had been distributed throughout the Air Service in penny numbers but for some time, men like Boelcke had been arguing that specialised 'hunting' squadrons, each consisting of around fourteen fighters, should be formed to carry the fight over into the skies above the British and French lines. In 1916, these ideas were given their trial and Boelcke was given the task of forming one of the first Jagdstaffeln (hunting squadrons).

Boelcke was an inspiration in the Service and aspiring fighter pilots longed to serve under him. He knew that he would need a particular type of pilot for his Staffel and he set out to pick men whom he thought had the necessary qualities: enthusiasm, aggression and team spirit. Manfred von Richthofen was still flying bombers over Russia when Boelcke visited the east to see his brother. When Boelcke asked Richthofen to join his new squadron and become a fighter pilot he was overjoyed, for now he could fly *and* hunt the enemy; there was nothing finer for a young cavalry officer.

Boelcke commanded Jagdstaffel 2 at Bertincourt; he had hand-picked the pilots and intended them to be an élite unit and an effective testimony to his ideas about aerial combat. To be effective, any military unit must be a cohesive team and it must be properly led. Boelcke was an expert leader: he knew instinctively how to inspire loyalty, how to bind his pilots together, making them proud of their unit, proud of themselves, making it a matter of honour never to let each other, or the squadron, down. He was also an expert teacher and tactician and he spent days instilling his pilots with his principles of air combat: stick together in close formation; seek some advantage before engaging the enemy; get behind and close before firing; if the enemy dives to attack you, don't fly away, meet him head-on. By September 1916 the squadron was ready in spirit and on the 16th they were equipped with the latest single-seater fighter, the Albatros D.II. The pilots were itching to try them out as soon as they arrived.

They took off at dawn and headed west. Over Cambrai they found a flight of F.E.2bs. Boelcke manoeuvred the squadron between the British flight and their own lines, cutting off their retreat. Then he aimed his whole team at them, going for the leader himself. Richthofen selected his target and disciplined himself to carry out Boelcke's instructions. They were below and he held his fire as the F.E.2 grew bigger and bigger in his sights, feeling his way into the F.E.2's blind spot. Then he opened fire. The observer fired back while the pilot twisted and turned, trying to prevent Richthofen from getting on to his tail, clearly no novice. The F.E.2 had a manoeuvrable machine-gun whereas the Albatros had to fire in the direction it was flying so they flew round in circles, each waiting for the other to make a small mistake. Eventually the British pilot did and Richthofen got in a burst of fire at very close range. He hit the engine, the F.E.2 swayed from side to side, then glided down to a forced landing in a field on the German side of the lines. Richthofen was ecstatic. He landed in the same field and went over to the shot-up British machine. Soldiers were lifting the crew out as he arrived: the observer, Lieutenant Rees, was dead, and the pilot, Lieutenant Morris, died on the way to hospital.

Back at the squadron, there was general rejoicing: Boelcke, Reimann, Boehme and Richthofen had all scored. There was a macabre side to Richthofen's sense of honour: he had a headstone erected to the two British airmen at the site of their landing and he ordered a silver goblet from a silversmith in Berlin inscribed with the date of his first official aerial victory. In the four weeks which followed, he shot down six more aircraft and each time he ordered a new silver goblet. His trophies were not confined to goblets, he visited the crash sites of as many of his victims as he could and collected a souvenir from each, a machine-gun here, a charred fabric cockade there. But the trophy he desired most of all, the medal he longed to wear, was the 'Pour le Mérite'.

On 28 October, the squadron came across two isolated British aircraft. Boelcke signalled and six Albatroses streamed after him into the attack. In the heat of the battle, Erwin Boehme, flying on Boelcke's wingtip, touched Boelcke's aircraft, the wings buckled and Boelcke spiralled down instantly.

The squadron and all Germany went into mourning; their leader and hero was dead. His aggression had been infectious and the example of his type of leadership was vital to the type of unit he had created. The squadron was named after its fallen leader – Jagdstaffel Boelcke.

Richthofen gradually built up his score and each time he shot down an opponent, he ordered another silver goblet. His eleventh victory was against a very tough opponent – a D.H.2 – and as soon as they began tangling, Richthofen knew that he was up against an expert. They flew so close to each other at times, jockeying for position, that Richthofen could see his opponent's head movements and at one point, the Englishman waved to him. Both men held their fire, but the advantage was with Richthofen because the wind was blowing the duelling pair further and further across the lines into German-occupied territory and as they fought, so they gradually lost altitude. A hundred feet above the ground, the RFC pilot had no alternative but to head for home and set off as fast as he could on a zigzag course. But Richthofen could now get right behind him, and just short of the lines he fired a sustained burst and the D.H.2 crashed. The pilot was one of Britain's aces of the time, Major Lanoe Hawker, VC, DSO, known to the Germans as 'the English Boelcke'. Richthofen was extremely proud to have shot him down and when he retrieved Hawker's machine-gun as a souvenir from the wreckage, it was given a place of honour above the door in his room.

On 16 January 1917 he shot down his sixteenth aircraft and reached a long and cherished ambition – he was now the leading German fighter ace by score. Earlier in the war, the 'Pour le

Mérite' was awarded for fewer kills and Richthofen was extremely anxious to have the decoration. Two days later, he was awarded the coveted medal and given command of a Jagdstaffel, No. 11.

By comparison with Jagdstaffel Boelcke, Jasta 11 was a rudderless outfit. The two units had been in existence more or less the same length of time when Richthofen took it over but it still had only a single, unconfirmed victory to its credit. Richthofen personally doubled the score the day after he arrived and trebled it the day after that. Leadership flowered almost effortlessly in him. He set about welding the men into a real fighting unit; he would be their teacher as Boelcke had been his. He spent hours on the ground in deep discussion with the pilots, going over their battles, criticising them and encouraging them in long sessions. The competition was fierce and Richthofen saw to it that his new command's score began to mount steadily.

The transformation of Jasta 11 was an extraordinary testimony to Richthofen's leadership. By mid-April 1917, 'Bloody April' for the RFC, its pilots had shot down over a hundred aircraft. The British lost 150 aircraft in a month, of which Richthofen shot down 21. His brother Lothar had joined the squadron and he shot down the British 'ace of aces', Captain Albert Ball of 56 Squadron. The qualities which distinguish an 'ace' from the 'ordinary' fighter pilots are a curious mixture – he needs to believe utterly in his own invincibility, he must be a marksman with his aircraft, using it as a gun, he must see combat through to a kill. In his early fights, Richthofen waited to see *if* his opponent fell when he fired, but soon he developed a *will* to bring him down – 'he must fall' became the Richthofen dictum. And for him they did. He was utterly confident of his own superiority as a German and of his own personal courage over his opponent. Personal courage, he said, was the decisive factor in victory. He was a born hunter and in a rather patronising summing-up of the qualities of his French and British counterparts, he might have been discussing the relative merits of hunting different types of wild game. The British, though 'impudent', were, he allowed, 'plucky fellows' and never flinched when he shot at them. They were 'sporting', a quality he rather admired and saw as rooted in their Germanic origins. The French, on the other hand, were 'sneaky', they preferred to hide and set a trap for the unwary, and since only the inexperienced German 'hunter' would fall for such a thing they were not to be feared as much; they were more like 'carbonated water' in a fight, a fizz of rage followed quickly by flatness.

The German Air Service and the RFC had different approaches to the matter of 'aces'; the German High Command deliberately cultivated Richthofen as a popular figure and started what became one of the most durable legends in military aviation, the legend of the 'Red Baron'. He was a baron by birth but he was dubbed the Red Baron because of the blood-red colour of his aircraft. The drabness of camouflage was not his style, he had his entire machine painted red. At the outset, it was for no particular reason (except possibly sheer flamboyance) but later on he realised its value as a morale-building feature and he also used it to be easily recognised in the air.

The Royal Flying Corps cultivated the aggression of its individual pilots in line with its overall policy of going on to the offensive, but the higher levels of the service were set firmly against such publicity, seeing it as invidious to select individuals for special praise in what was a team effort. Mick Mannock, Britain's leading ace with 74 victories, was hardly known outside the RFC.

By 1917, the RFC was a much larger organisation, with possibly less time for such considerations. Its size and effectiveness was what worried the German High Command, for though their pilots like Richthofen might shoot down dozens of aircraft, the RFC kept up a relentless pressure.

In May 1917, Richthofen flew to Kreuznach for discussions with the senior commanders. After his polite breakfast with the Kaiser he had discussions with his superiors and after some leave, returned for the Front again. The German High Command had developed some new tactics: first, they sent Gotha bombers across the Channel to bomb England, hoping to draw off some of the RFC's fighter strength from France, and secondly, they formed the first Jagdgeschwader, a fighter group of four Jastas, fifty aircraft, all under one commander. The concept behind it was to have a powerful, effective, élite unit with its own ground transport and portable accommodation so that it could be flexible and move about the front as and where it was most needed. The man to lead the first Geschwader was the Red Baron.

It had not been operating long before it was given the nickname 'Flying Circus'. The pilots' tented, nomadic existence had an air of the travelling circus and they took their cue from their leader and painted their aircraft in garish colours. To many observers, the colourful aeroplanes, the bizarre souvenirs and the extravagant lifestyles which men such as Richthofen adopted and cultivated within their units were sheer flamboyance. But there was a purpose behind them: binding men together, giving them an identity as a unit and a pride in that unit, is fundamental to creating an effective fighting force. With the extraordinary task imposed on fighter pilots in the First World War, extraordinary means had to be found to generate that esprit that made for fighting effectiveness. Richthofen found the means and it paid off in the air: some of the best pilots wanted to join the Flying Circus and serve with Richthofen; once they were in, and so highly motivated, they became an extremely effective fighting force. He was, too, a leader by example, always taking his place in the fighting, always taking the same risks as the men he led. The legend of the Red Baron became a powerful force in the air battle and it was reinforced each time the Circus or Richthofen himself scored.

On 6 July 1917, he attacked a British two-seater. As he approached, the British gunner opened up at about three hundred yards, far too far away to be effective. Richthofen decided to wait and let him waste ammunition. Suddenly he felt a blow on the side of his head as a bullet ploughed through the side of his scalp, blinding him and paralysing him. The Albatros went into a dive. Richthofen was conscious, and though he realised that he was plunging downwards, there was little he could do until he regained the use of his limbs and eyes. He willed himself back into action. His limbs recovered first and he managed to switch off the fuel and ignition, reducing the chances of fire. Spots appeared before his eyes and gradually he regained some sight; he peered closely at the altimeter and was able to make out that he was at 2500 feet. He managed to level out and restart the engine but felt so faint that he decided to land as quickly as possible anywhere he could. Members of the squadron had followed him down and were protecting him against any further attack, but the landing was a fearful one; he took telegraph wires and poles with him before sliding to a halt. He did not have the strength to get out of the cockpit and sat there until some soldiers came up and put a dressing on his head, then took him to hospital.

All the time he was away from the Circus he wanted to get back. Even as a sick man, he felt that his presence was vital at the Front and he felt lost, too, without the closeness of the comradeship. He wanted his philosophy and tactics to be carried through in the air. There was an alternative way of patrolling an area – flying through it as often as possible on a patrol, denying access to the enemy observation aircraft. But he favoured the aggressive approach, flying out to meet the enemy and shoot him down. He quoted the great German military theorist, Clausewitz, in support of his persistence, declaring that nothing else mattered but the destruction of the opposition. Mastery of the air, he felt, would come only by overcoming the enemy in combat, not by flying standing patrols. He was away for a month and when he got back he went straight into the fighting. But he was still weak and on several occasions he had to be carried from his aircraft after landing.

The High Command was extremely reluctant to see him killed, especially if he was killed simply because he could not take the physical strain. They felt that his death would have a deeply damaging effect on morale well beyond the Air Service. He was a symbol of the German warrior tradition and too valuable to risk in the battle.

He could have given up fighting at any time and there were many people who advised him to do so, but as a man of honour the prospect of a staff job, away from the battle, or even worse, away from the war on some public relations exercise, was something he refused to contemplate. He could not bear to have it thought that he had left the fighting to others, and these sentiments he extended beyond the fraternity of the Air Service to the soldiers in the trenches whose courage and endurance he was always at pains to recognise.

Eventually, after he had made his sixtieth kill and the Kaiser had intervened to offer him some hunting on his personal estates in East Prussia, he agreed to take a rest.

While he was on leave he wrote *Der Rote Kampfflieger* (*The Red Fighter Pilot*). As an account of his experiences, it is written with a haughty understatement; the style is frequently more revealing than the content. It starts with a cheerful indifference to war, even though he was clearly aware of the crudeness which surrounded him. There is never even a hint that Germany might lose. He is very open about his ambitions – to get the Blue Max, to be the top-scoring pilot, etc – and he refers frequently to his own physical courage simply as a matter of fact. In the early pages, the deaths of comrades are recorded heroically and with sublime lack of emotion. Towards the end, however, he begins to be more reflective and the death of friends, particularly, evinces the saddest of sentiments.

But nothing could keep him away; the lure of the battle, the need to be where it was happening, was as strong for him as it was for the aces on both sides. In November 1917 he was back. It was the month when massed tanks were used for the first time. On the 20th the British launched an offensive at Cambrai in terrible weather. Tanks, with infantry following behind, broke through the German lines while above them, sandwiched between the ground and low clouds, dodging trees and telegraph poles, RFC pilots supported them by machine-gunning the German positions. The attack started successfully and the British did considerable damage behind the German lines. It also caused panic in the German headquarters: the Richthofen Circus was summoned to take on the low-flying aircraft and moved to airfields nearer to the battle to support the local Jasta which was also put under Richthofen's command. Early in the morning, they took off and flew in low over the battlefield looking for the enemy. It was different from the dogfighting which they were used to, high in a generally cloudless sky; the pilots on both sides spent much of the time in a deadly game of hide-and-seek, searching for each other in a misty, drizzle-soaked sky, preoccupied most of the time with avoiding collisions.

On 30 November, the Germans launched a successful counterattack and the Circus provided low-level cover; in the fight, Richthofen scored his sixty-third victory. But there were no more silver goblets; after his sixtieth victory, economic conditions in Germany were such that silver was no longer available.

As commander of such a complex unit flying regularly in combat, Richthofen led an extremely busy life. He was still only a captain, but he was a bright star in an otherwise rather drab firmament. He was more widely known and admired than most of the generals above him and he had to endure a steady stream of official visitors to his headquarters. It was an added burden and he professed a strong dislike for publicity, but he cooperated because he understood its importance in building morale both within the Army and on the home front. Honours were showered on him, not only from Imperial Germany but from her allies Austria, Bulgaria and Turkey as well.

The winter was a relatively quiet time for airmen because of the weather. But it was a busy time for commanders such as Richthofen because the German High Command was planning a spring offensive, attacking the British where they were weakest and driving a wedge between the British and the French. Richthofen spent hours visiting airfields and planning his Geschwader's part in the offensive, training his pilots, getting to know them and finding the right junior commanders. He swapped his Albatros for one of the new Fokker Dr.1 triplanes, a fast and highly manoeuvrable machine which, once it was his, he had painted bright red.

The offensive began on 21 March 1918 and initially it advanced successfully. As the Front moved, so aircraft moved with it, and soon they were operating from airfields captured from the British. The aerial battle was fierce and Richthofen's Circus was constantly in the battle: in March and April, the British lost around a thousand aircraft; Richthofen's personal score rose into the seventies.

He was the undisputed top fighter pilot on either side and that spring, for a time at least, it appeared that his side was winning. But his own spirits were low: there was little left of the carefree young officer who had gone to war in 1914. When he landed now after a fight there was a feeling of accomplishment and duty done, but inwardly he felt wretched. He was physically exhausted and it showed in his dark-ringed eyes. He was liable to become depressed. When he did, he hid himself away in his quarters, surrounded by his trophies; wherever he went and whatever his surroundings, Lanoe Hawker's machine-gun still hung above his door. Deep down, even during the offensive, he knew that whatever the individual efforts of people like him and his pilots, Germany could not make the effort needed to win.

On 20 April, Richthofen shot down his seventy-ninth and eightieth victims and that night he celebrated passing the eighty mark.

On the morning of the 21st, he took off from his base at Cappy with a flight of six, to patrol over the Somme area. He had his young cousin in the flight, who had not experienced air combat before and was under strict instructions not to get involved in any fighting.

At around the same time, just twenty odd miles away across the lines at Bertangles, a flight of Sopwith Camels took off under the command of Captain Roy Brown, a Canadian serving with the recently-formed RAF. In his flight was an old schoolfriend of Brown's, Captain May, who was also very inexperienced and under the same instructions as Richthofen's cousin.

The two flights met in the air. Brown went to the aid of two British reconnaissance aircraft which had come under attack from one of Richthofen's flights. It was one of the fiercest battles Brown had been in and for a time he thought that he was unlikely to get out of it alive. Out of the corner of his eye, he thought he saw May shoot down one of the enemy, then head for home. In fact, it was Richthofen's cousin who was flying away from the battle as ordered. Suddenly a red triplane went after May. Brown managed to break off the fight after a struggle and went in pursuit, determined to help his friend.

The pilot of the triplane was Manfred von Richthofen and he was about to make May his eighty-first victim. Brown was above and behind him and dived in an instinctive attack and fired, raking Richthofen's aircraft along the fuselage. Richthofen turned his head to see his attacker, then died almost immediately.

His aircraft crashed near the lines. Once the identity of the pilot became known on the ground, souvenir-hunters arrived and stripped it bare.

There was a profound respect for Richthofen among Allied pilots and Germany's supreme hero was given a funeral worthy of the greatest airman of the war. It was a sombre and stately occasion: he lay on a dais inside a marquee, surrounded by wreaths brought by airmen from bases all around. They came to pay their respects and they came out of sheer curiosity, to see the man whose name was synonymous with fighting prowess in the air. Then he was buried with full military ceremony in the little churchyard at Bertangles, his coffin carried to the grave by six RAF squadron commanders, all of whom had been decorated for bravery. An account of the proceedings was sent to his parents.

His mother, the Baroness von Richthofen, turned some of the rooms at Schweidnitz into a museum where the Red Baron's trophies, his silver goblets, his cherished pieces of crashed British aircraft were displayed: Major Lanoe Hawker's machine-gun was given a place of honour. When Manfred's younger brother Lothar, who had also been an ace and served in the Circus, was killed in an aircraft crash in 1922 his memorabilia were included and Schweidnitz became something of a shrine for wartime pilots from both sides.

The legend of the Red Baron would not die, if anything it grew as time passed. In 1925, his body was brought back from France, accompanied by his youngest brother Bolko with a group of ex-wartime fighter pilots. It was carried by train in an open carriage on a triumphal journey: church bells rang, crowds gathered wherever the train stopped and patriotic songs were sung. His mother wanted him to be reburied in Schweidnitz but she gave way to the popular demand for a place of honour in Berlin and the pomp of a state funeral.

After his death he was given the same honour as his mentor Boelcke – his Jagdstaffel, No. 11, was named after him. They fought on through the last months of the war as Jagdstaffel Richthofen. As part of the Armistice, Germany was forbidden to retain her military aircraft and on 16 November 1918, the pilots flew their machines to Strasbourg and surrendered them to the

French authorities. For a time, that was the end of the Richthofen Squadron. But it was too powerful a military legend to die – Hermann Goering himself had served in it during the First World War – and when the Luftwaffe was formed it was revived again. After the Second World War, when the new German Air Force was formed, it was revived yet again and today there is still a Richthofen Squadron.

7   Charles Lindbergh

The North Atlantic is a moody and generally bad-tempered ocean. Its character reflects the brutality of the storms which roll down from the Arctic to batter their way across the thousands of miles of emptiness; massive, growling seas, towering pillars of cloud full of swirling ice crystals, all whipped into a frenzy by fearsome winds. It was like that in early May 1927 when three aviators were each preparing to become the first to fly across the great ocean from New York to Paris and to win the Orteig Prize of $25,000.

The storms began to break on 19 May, but after a week of rain, the surface of Roosevelt Field, Long Island, was soggy and the night was bathed in soft drizzle. There were puddles along the runway and they reflected in the headlamps of a motorcar as it towed an aircraft, tail-first, towards the take-off point. Chattering spectators followed its slow progress; every now and then they were dazzled by a photographer's flashbulb. On the nose of the aircraft, its name was painted in black letters – *The Spirit of St Louis*.

As dawn broke, the aircraft was ready at the west end of the runway and a tall, lean figure of boyish appearance arrived. His name was Charles Lindbergh. He climbed into the cockpit. It was a tense moment; a murmur of excitement rippled round the crowd. The mechanics and helpers stood back – he was going to try it.

The atmosphere was spiced with a special frisson, the thought that these could be Lindbergh's last moments of life thrilled the spectators; the previous year, only a few yards from the spot where *The Spirit of St Louis* stood, two men had been killed attempting the same flight. They had burned to death in their overloaded aircraft which burst into flames after failing to lift off the runway. The onlookers knew that they were about to witness a triumph or another spectacular tragedy. To add to the drama of the occasion, just ten days previously two French aviators had disappeared into the Atlantic trying to make the crossing in the opposite direction.

In the cockpit, Lindbergh opened the throttle to full power. The aircraft strained against the chocked wheels and whipped the drizzle into a fine spray. He looked at the quivering needle of the rev counter. It showed thirty revolutions below normal – the effect of the damp weather. Lindbergh paused for thought: with the full load of fuel the aircraft was heavier than ever before; the runway was soft and there was a slight deficiency in power; there were men spaced out down the runway with fire extinguishers and another in a car ready to race alongside him. He was keyed up and longing to be on his own, to get away from the crowds and the photographers. He decided to go.

He signalled his intention: the chocks were taken away, he opened the throttle wide again and with the help of men pushing on the wing-struts the aircraft began to roll slowly forward. After what seemed an age, the men fell behind; he was gathering speed. Now he could feel some response in the controls but they were still sluggish. More speed, more speed: past the halfway mark now, no turning back; he would fly or crash. The controls stiffened, he held the aircraft down on the runway, waiting until it was really ready to fly, and then eased back very gently. The wheels gave a final shove against the earth, the controls felt very heavy, but he was airborne. It was just before eight o'clock in the morning on 20 May 1927.

Almost every newspaper and radio station in America and many more around the world picked up the story. Readers and listeners were hungry for every scrap of news of his progress and when he was sighted for the last time, over Newfoundland, heading out into the mighty Atlantic, interest built up to fever pitch.

After thirty-three hours alone in the air he landed in Paris. He had taken off as a relatively obscure mail pilot; he landed the greatest hero in the world. He left America a solitary man with an uncomplicated private life; from the moment he landed his life became a saga of controversy. A very private man, he became public property, the object of mass adulation and running battles with the press. It was not entirely for what he had done, his fame was the product of the curious chemistry between the flippancy of the age and the steadfastness of his own character and the some-times curious way he conducted himself.

He was, and remains, the greatest hero aviation has ever had.

Charles Augustus Lindbergh Jnr was born in Detroit, in the bosom of his mother's family, on 4 February 1902. Within a few weeks he was moved to Little Falls, Minnesota, to the house his father had built in a private wilderness on the banks of the Mississippi.

Charles Augustus Lindbergh Snr was a lawyer, but the passion in his life was politics, the politics of reform. It was a zeal he had inherited from his own father, Ola Mannson, a rugged individualist of indomitable personal courage and conviction. Mannson had represented the interests of small farmers in the Swedish Parliament before changing the family name and emigrating to America in 1859. He went to America to get away from the rigid social and economic systems in Europe and to make the long trail west to carve out new lives on new farms on the prairies.

The focus of Lindbergh Snr's politics was the economic relationship between 'big business' and the small man. The way he saw things, banks, insurance companies and finance houses soaked up the farmers' savings from areas such as rural Minnesota and instead of investing it back into the area, placed it wherever they could make the greatest profit. He tried to organise local, cooperative investment schemes in Minnesota, but they failed. In 1906 he ran for Congress on the Republican ticket (even though his radical and reformist views made him rather an unorthodox Republican), and was elected, principally on his strong personal popularity and local connections.

Charles Lindbergh's mother was his father's second wife, his first wife having died after an operation. Evangeline Lindbergh came from a scientifically orientated family. She was a graduate from the University of Michigan and she met her husband when she was teaching science at the Little Falls High School. It was not a happy marriage, they were both strong-willed and of contrasting natures and shortly after the birth of their only child, Charles Jnr, they became permanently estranged. There was no question of divorce but they lived separate lives. On the surface life went on as normal; both mother and father were in complete control of their emotions and showed nothing of their estrangement and the unhappiness it must have generated.

His early life was split between his parents, though he spent most of his time in Little Falls or Detroit with his mother. His maternal grandfather and great-uncle both kept laboratories and the young Charles was free to roam and have the mysteries of science explained with the aid of medical specimens and technical apparatus. Sometimes he went to Washington with his father and when his father was at home they went on camping trips into the wilderness along the Mississippi. On these trips, his father encouraged him to be independently minded, physically tough and self-reliant.

His father's career was a controversial one and Charles was able to see the turbulence of American politics at first-hand. Congressman Lindbergh persistently harried big-business interests and made plenty of enemies both in politics and the press. He campaigned for, and got, an investigation into the excessive influence which a few financiers exerted over the economy and was vindicated by the Congressional Committee which reported. He was fervent in his opposition to America's involvement in the First World War. He vigorously represented the interests of his constituents in Minnesota, but his personal convictions led him to espouse unpopular causes. When it was suggested that the Catholic Church might exert too great an influence over schools, the press and individual liberties, he once again called for an impartial investigation. This time the system ensnared him: he was portrayed as anti-Catholic and satirised and ridiculed in the newspapers and when he ran for the Senate in 1916 he was defeated.

Charles accompanied his father on electoral campaigns, not so much because of an infant interest in politics but because it gave him a chance to drive the family car to which he was devoted. He loved tinkering with mechanical things and in 1916, he drove his mother and an uncle on a five-week trip over the roughest of roads from Minnesota to California, doing all the driving and looking after the car himself. He was fourteen. Back in Little Falls, he bought a motorcycle.

At school he was a poor student and, through a special provision to keep people on the land in support of the war effort, he was able to graduate early without finishing high school and take over the family farm with his mother. He was a hard-working farmer but his heart was elsewhere. He read the stories of the air-war in France and longed to fly. His mother and father were at one in their opposition to flying, and his father was passionately against the war, so Charles had to cherish the idea of becoming a fighter pilot quietly.

He wanted to give up farming and saw a way out by agreeing to his parents' wish that he go to college. In the autumn of 1920, he and his mother moved to Madison so that he could study mechanical engineering at the University of Wisconsin. At college he was an outsider; except for one or two other engineering freshmen he cared little for the company of his fellow students and even less for any girls – he spent his time between classes engaged in his own experiments and developing a taste for dangerous pursuits.

The conquest of fear had a cathartic effect on him, purging

pent-up energy and emotions in one exhilarating moment of challenge, risk and ultimate proof of his own fearlessness. Near the college was a steep hill which ran down to a T-junction with a cross street. On the opposite side of the cross street was a high wall. He discussed the chances of a motorcyclist making it into the cross street before hitting the wall after a brake failure on the hill. Friends said it couldn't be done; he disagreed and went to fetch his motorbike. He rode to the top of the hill and accelerated down the slope without touching the brakes; his friends watched horrified as the speed increased and it looked as if he was going to finish up against the wall. He didn't, because the bike crashed into the gutter first and Lindbergh was thrown along the road. He picked himself up, retrieved his bike, then roared back up the hill again to repeat the performance. This time, as he hurtled down and began to lean into the curve, he gunned the engine, kicking the back wheel round, just managing to avoid the gutter.

He was idling at college, his whole spirit yearned to be doing something more exciting. His mother was set on his achieving a college education, but it was no great surprise when in April 1922 he told her that he was leaving. The conquest of any outward display of emotional feeling was a family trait and she showed little emotion at his departure but inwardly she must have been heartbroken and he must have known it. Not only was he giving up college, not only was he clearly leaving the close relationship they had had all his life, he was leaving it for the most dangerous profession – flying.

He had seen an advertisement for flying tuition by the Nebraska Aircraft Company for purchasers of their Lincoln Standard aircraft. He wrote off pointing out that he could not buy an aircraft but he could pay for instruction. When they agreed to take him on he left for Nebraska immediately. Unknown to him, the company was in the most frightful financial mess, so, when Reg Page, the director, asked for $500 in advance, he paid up. Ira Biffle, his instructor, was a good pilot and a tough instructor but he was an unreliable character and frequently left the young and eager Charles Lindbergh for days without a lesson. His first flight in an aeroplane was on 9 April 1922. In the following month, after another eight hours of instruction, he was ready to go solo, but it then transpired that the instructional machine, a Lincoln Standard, was about to be sold and Reg Page quite reasonably pointed out that he could not risk such a valuable asset in the hands of a novice. The aircraft was sold to Erold Dahl, a barnstorming pilot, and since Biffle had left the company too, there was no instructor either. It was useless trying to get the money he was owed out of Page and he was unwilling to admit defeat and go back to his mother, so he begged Dahl to take him along on the barnstorming trip. After initial reluctance Dahl agreed.

After the grim years of the Great War, the world, and in particular America, entered on a period when grossly superficial values were in fashion. The decade took its name from the mood of the times – the 'Roaring Twenties'. It was a time of bizarre entertainment; cheap thrills were the rage, and the newest, 'thrillingest' thing was the aeroplane. 'Barnstorming' and 'Flying Circus' were among the words coined to describe the spectacles which pilots put on for the crowds. Ex-wartime fighter pilots re-enacted their battles for a fee; freelances toured the country, attending fairs, shows, any occasion where they could attract a crowd or find a sponsor by performing hair-raising stunts. It was about the most dangerous and uncomfortable way to earn a living which had ever been devised: wing-walking, parachuting and aerobatics came first, then the spectators were encouraged to take 'joy rides' at $5 a time.

There was little money in the business and Charles Lindbergh had agreed to pay his own expenses for the trip, but he entered into the life with gusto, suggesting stunts to Dahl in which he, Lindbergh, walked out on the wing while they stunted over a town. It was a perfect opportunity to test his ability to overcome fear and to demonstrate it. He wanted to be part of the act, never part of the crowd; he was a doer, not a looker-on. He was so useful that Dahl agreed to pay his expenses and occasionally he let him fly the aircraft between destinations.

When the tour was over, they flew back to the Nebraska Aircraft Company. Page was still trying to keep the business alive, and to publicise the airfield, he had hired a stunt parachutist called Charlie Hardin. (Hardin's wife, a former circus trapeze-artiste, did wing-walking and sometimes she hung between the wheels of an aircraft by her teeth.) Unable to pursue his chosen career as a pilot for the moment, Lindbergh asked Hardin to let him try stunt-parachuting. He wanted to make his first jump as a stunt, imitating Hardin's act of a 'double jump' in which the jumper cut himself free from the parachute after leaving the aircraft, then fell again until checked by a second 'chute. At first Hardin said no, but when Lindbergh hinted that he might buy a parachute, Hardin finally agreed.

In those days a parachute wasn't strapped to the jumper, it was secured to the struts between the wings of the aircraft by a slip-knot and he had to crawl along the wing without it and hook himself up before jumping. The day arrived and an aircraft took Lindbergh up to 2000 feet. He climbed out of the cockpit into the blast of the slipstream and crawled along the wing. When he had hooked up, the pilot signalled and throttled back; Lindbergh pulled the line to the slip-knot and fell suddenly, dragging the parachute out of its package. It opened immediately and he reached up with a knife and cut himself free. Then things went wrong: the second parachute should have opened immediately but it stubbornly stayed packed. On the ground Hardin and Page watched horrified as Lindbergh fell like a stone; the line which attached one parachute to the other, allowing one to pull out the other, had broken too soon. Eventually it did emerge from the pack and blossomed slowly and only just in time. Lindbergh's exhilaration was complete: he had done it with only the smallest margin of safety.

He bought a parachute from Charlie Hardin and then teamed up with another stunt pilot, a man called Lynch, in July, for a late summer barnstorming trip. Barnstorming was a life of relentless activity: flying between engagements, living rough and taking little in the way of comforts or personal possessions. They flew through the western states – Kansas, Wyoming, Colorado, Nebraska – and in between shows Lindbergh did some of the flying, slowly increasing his experience at the controls. They scattered leaflets over the towns, publicising themselves as 'Cupid' Lynch and 'Daredevil' Lindbergh; Lynch did the stunting, Lindbergh made the parachute jumps and on one occasion, Lindbergh stood on the wing while Lynch flew a loop. But barnstorming was strictly a summer occupation and when the trip ended at Billings, Montana, in October 1922 there was nothing else for him to do except go back to Little Falls for the winter.

His motorcycle was at Lincoln and he set off to collect it in a characteristically adventurous way, buying a boat to take him down the Yellowstone River to the Missouri. After a couple of days' hammering on the rocks, the boat began to leak and he was forced to finish the journey by rail.

He spent the winter either on the farm (the land had been leased to a local man) or with his father in Minneapolis. His father was dead against his son's flying career, but having always encouraged him to be independent in mind and deed he found it difficult to argue too strongly against what his son wanted to do. In the end, he even agreed to guarantee a loan with a Little Falls bank so that Charles could buy his own aeroplane.

The following spring, in April 1923, he paid $500 for a rather forlorn-looking, but mechanically sound, Curtiss Jenny at Souther Field, Alabama, where the Army sold its surplus aircraft by auction. He had never flown solo, he had not flown at all since the previous October and that was on a different type of aircraft; however, since no licence was required and he owned the aircraft he carefully neglected to tell anybody of his lack of experience and decided to fly his first solo there and then.

He decided to do a couple of ground runs first, not lifting off, just to get the feel of the new machine. It was different from the Lincoln Standard, livelier, and it leapt into the air sooner than he expected. When he tried to put it gently back on the ground again, it bounced heavily back into the air. After a series of teeth-rattling bounces he finally landed in one piece but only after narrowly avoiding a crash. He taxied back to the hangars, rather ashamed of himself. Fortunately, a sympathetic local pilot had seen the performance and offered to take him up for a few circuits before he went solo and Charles, shamefaced but eager, readily agreed. After giving the eager pupil a little instruction on the Jenny, the stranger suggested that he wait until evening when the air was still and then go by himself.

That evening he took off alone for the first time. Not content with a circuit or two, he flew up high, bursting with pride and exhilaration as he looked down on the vast expanse of Alabama. The whole of the US was now open to him; he could go where he liked; it was his own aircraft and he was alone flying it. He had never landed alone before but as the shadows darkened the now deserted airfield, he glided in to land without difficulty. He was a pilot.

That summer he was an aviating busker, a gypsy, often sleeping rough, under his aircraft's wing, servicing his own engine, barnstorming and giving joy rides on his own account. Life was great: he really was part of the rootless aviation fraternity and he enjoyed the company of the rugged individuals, the swaggering and energetic band of devoted flyers who lived the same way.

He left the barnstorming circuit briefly to help his father who was trying to get back into national politics. The attraction of an aeroplane might help to build an audience for the ageing politician. The first time he took his father for a flight, they planned to drop campaign leaflets over a town. Lindbergh Snr held the bundle and when his son signalled he threw them all over the side at once. They thudded against the tailplane, causing some consternation on board, and only covered a small part of the town. On another occasion they crashed on take-off: Lindbergh Snr was injured and Charles was sure that somebody had tampered with the aircraft. Either way his father decided that his path to the Senate would be smoother without the aid of his son's aeroplane. He never did make it into the Senate; the following year he died of a brain tumour.

Charles took his mother flying too. She was living in Detroit and teaching science and during the school holidays she went on a barnstorming tour with him, helping him with publicity and touting for joy-ride business.

Barnstorming was great fun, but it was seasonal, dangerous and financially unrewarding. Like many pilots, Lindbergh was convinced that the era of commercial aviation was dawning, with passenger and mail services which could operate with speed and reliability. He wanted to be part of it, a real professional rather than part of what was clearly a passing phase in aviation more closely linked to show-business. He went to the 1923 National Air Races at Lambert Field, St Louis, where he met Marvin Northrop, the aircraft designer. Lindbergh explained his desire to get into serious aviation and Northrop advised him to be patient and in the meantime join the Army Air Corps where he would get a wider and very thorough training. Lindbergh did not really want to be a career soldier, but, as Northrop pointed out, he could fly to his heart's content in training, learn an enormous amount about the technical side and then opt to serve on the reserve. Since there was no immediate sign of commercial aviation opening up he decided to give up his wandering, and rather aimless, existence and join the Army.

The training was long, intensive and thorough; with his stunt-flying experience, he was a natural as a fighter pilot and he spent many hours happily practising formation flying, aerial gunnery and fighting tactics at the government's expense. Unlike his poor record at college, he responded to the Army's training with enthusiasm and when he was awarded his wings in the spring of 1925, he was top of a class of eighteen which had started out with 104. His flying career and his life were nearly ended just before he finished his training, when he had a crash. He was flying an S.E.5, practising a formation attack on a D.H.4, and in the mock battle he collided with another S.E.5 and the two aircraft fell, locked together. His great presence of mind and coolness in dangerous pursuits saved him; he just managed to extricate himself from the tumbling wreckage and land safely by parachute. Once qualified he went straight on to the reserve and started looking for a job.

The US Post Office was planning to introduce an airmail service and companies were to bid for sections of it. Back in St Louis, Lindbergh met two brothers, Bill and Frank Robertson, who were bidding for the St Louis–Chicago sector. If they were successful they would need pilots and, with his experience and his army training, they promised to hire him if they got the contract.

In the meantime he had to look elsewhere. He could not return to freelancing as a barnstormer because he had sold the Jenny, so he went to work for a barnstorming company who were offering a very high salary. In the nature of its attraction to the crowds, barnstorming had to keep finding new ways to thrill people and for his salary of $400 a month, Lindbergh had to fly at night, trailing a dazzling string of blazing fireworks. Fortunately for him, the Robertson brothers were awarded the mail contract soon afterwards and they sent for him.

On 15 April 1926 Charles Lindbergh made the inaugural flight on the St Louis to Chicago mail run. The job was not particularly well paid, for after an initial rush, the volume of letters slowed to a trickle and since the company was paid by the pound, the cashflow dwindled. But those struggling companies were the beginning of commercial aviation. Charles Lindbergh was determined to stick with it. The flying itself was undramatic and did not make the same kind of demands on the pilot as barnstorming – no more the split-second timing and high-speed passes close to the ground. In this job the skill came in being reliable and punctual at all times. One of the main dangers was the weather; weather forecasts were unreliable and pilots frequently finished up landing in farmers' fields waiting for the weather to clear. For Lindbergh, this element of danger was just there to be overcome. For him, the slogan 'the mail must get through' was no idle statement, it suited his single-mindedness of purpose perfectly to have such a clear aim and he made it an article of faith to get it through if humanly possible. In the summer, when the days were long and the weather relatively good, it was not so difficult but as the winter drew in, darkness and bad weather made it much more hazardous.

On an autumn evening in 1926 Lindbergh was flying the route which, by now, he knew like the back of his hand. All around, the sky was darkening and as he approached Chicago, a great bank of fog rolled off the Illinois River up to 800 to 1000 feet. From above, Lindbergh could see it stretching far ahead, so he decided to land somewhere until it cleared. The aircraft had a system to release a flare on a little parachute which illuminated the ground at night, but when he pulled the lever to drop it, it failed to operate.

Next he tried to fly high over the fog. As he climbed, he could make out the familiar shape of the city and its suburbs as the glow of their lights filtered through the grey blanket. On the ground below, unknown to him, mechanics were lighting petrol flares and shining a searchlight into the gloom but he never saw it. Next he examined the flare-release system again and found that the cable was slack. He decided to try another landing. As he turned west of the city the engine coughed and died; he switched to the reserve fuel tank and it caught again; he had twenty minutes to get down. He pulled the cable and the flare fell away and lit up the fog below which stretched as far as the light carried. He resigned himself to a parachute jump and started climbing to give himself as much height as possible. When the engine died again, he dived out of the cockpit and pulled the ripcord; soon he was floating serenely down towards the fog. Then he heard the unmistakable note of an aircraft approaching him; without his weight, the nose of his machine had tipped forward allowing the last drops of fuel to flow into the engine to restart it and now it was flying towards him, pilotless. After a few nervous seconds the engine note receded and he realised that the aircraft was spiralling down. Sure enough, the note increased and receded again as he sank into the fog bank. He landed in a field of high corn, picked up his parachute and walked across the fields until he found some tracks. They led to a farm where he met an astonished farmer who told him that an aircraft had crashed nearby.

'I'm the pilot,' Lindbergh told him.

At first the farmer didn't understand but after Lindbergh had assured him that he was fine and all he wanted to do was to find his aircraft, they set off through the foggy night. They found it about two miles away in a field where it had narrowly missed another farmhouse. Lindbergh retrieved the mail and took it to the nearest post office to go by rail. Such incidents certainly satisfied his lust for danger, just as the challenge of proving the reliability of aviation was met by keeping to the schedule of the mail flights, forced landings notwithstanding. But his being was still restless, he wanted to do more and he was always looking for new challenges.

In 1926 he heard of the Orteig Prize for the first time: $25,000 for a nonstop flight from New York to Paris or the shores of France. He was gripped by the challenge: it would be a huge advance in the demonstration of aviation as a viable means of international transport, it paid a lot more than flying the mail, and it offered danger. The dangerous element in such an enterprise was dramatically illustrated at Roosevelt Field, Long Island, on 20 September 1926.

All summer long the newspapers and the newsreels had been full of the story of Captain René Fonck, a French flying ace and war hero, who was going to attempt to fly the Atlantic in a specially modified Sikorsky S-35. The S-35 was a massive, three-engined machine designed as a future airliner. That autumn, it wasn't really ready for the attempt, the designer still wanted to carry out more tests, but there was a race on to win the Orteig Prize and when the weather cleared in late September, Fonck decided to go. He had a crew of four and when the S-35 was filled with 2500 gallons of fuel it weighed nearly 30,000 lbs, roughly 10,000 above its design weight. It was sheer hubris which led him and his team to make the attempt. When he opened up to full power, the overloaded aircraft accelerated only slowly at first, then it gradually built up. Moving fast, it hit a point where a road crossed the runway; a wheel flew off and it began to slew round; Fonck struggled with the controls and kept it straight, but by now he was committed to a take-off and could only hope that he would reach flying speed. The S-35 shot off the end of the runway, with even more pieces missing, and erupted into flame.

Fonck and his co-pilot, Curtin, scrambled clear but the radio operator and mechanic were burnt to death. Almost immediately, Sikorsky announced that he would build another aircraft and Fonck announced that he would fly it.

They were not the only competitors. In America there were two other teams, both supported by extensive funds. First there was Comdr Richard E. Byrd fresh from his triumphant flight over the North Pole; he had a Fokker Trimotor and was backed with $100,000 by the New York department-store tycoon, Rodman Wanamaker. Then there was Lt Comdr Noel Davis of the US Navy who had a specially adapted Pathfinder bomber backed by the American Legion. In France, another war ace, the debonair Charles Nungesser, was planning to fly in the opposite direction, against the prevailing winds, in a modified Levasseur PL8 naval aircraft. The two American entries were, like the Sikorsky, three-engined, multi-crewed machines; the French entry was big, but single-engined with an open cockpit for a crew of two. In late 1926 all three were under construction or modification.

Charles Lindbergh read the accounts of these preparations and he came to the conclusion that they were all trying to use aircraft which were not suited to the task, they were too big. Fonck's Sikorsky had demonstrated that: it had been furnished with seats, a divan, radios, all of which added to the weight. Lindbergh's approach was entirely the opposite, it was characteristically simple and relied heavily on him personally. He would fly alone, in a very spartan machine, saving every last ounce so that it could carry enough fuel to make the journey but would also be light enough to get off the ground in the first place. There was a machine which could do it, he felt sure: a one-off, single-engined prototype called the Wright/Bellanca, designed for the Wright Company to demonstrate their new Whirlwind engine.

That autumn Charles Lindbergh resolved to win the Orteig Prize. He had savings of around $2000, not nearly enough to buy the Wright/Bellanca but it was a start. He went to the businessmen of St Louis and sought their backing; some turned him away, especially when they heard that he was going to fly alone in a single-engined machine, but by late that year he had found a group of air-minded men who agreed to back him.

In November 1926 he went to New York to meet the Wright Company to see if they would sell him the Wright/Bellanca but they turned him down. Several weeks later he heard that it had been sold to a New York businessman called Levine. Through his contacts in the aviation world and the aviation press he searched for somebody who would build him an aircraft and came up with the names of a few companies which could do what he wanted – one of them was the Ryan Company of San Diego.

On 3 February 1927 he sent a telegram to the Ryan Company asking if they could build an aircraft to fly the Atlantic based on the Wright Whirlwind engine. They telegraphed back immediately; they could do it, at a cost of $6000 (plus the cost of the engine), and they could do it in three months.

Three days later Lindbergh received another telegram, this time from Bellanca, the designer of the Wright/Bellanca. He suggested that it would be worth coming to New York to discuss the possibility of buying the aircraft from its new owner, Levine. Lindbergh went to New York with a cheque for $15,000, eager to buy it. But Levine turned out to be a strange and slippery customer: he was prepared to sell the aircraft to Lindbergh and his backers, but he reserved the right to nominate the crew. Lindbergh was furious, either the aircraft was for sale or it wasn't. Levine would not budge, he clearly saw mileage in the publicity from any attempted flight and was equally clearly happy to use other people's money provided he could still control the enterprise and profit from it. Later on, Levine announced that the Wright/Bellanca would be flown across the Atlantic by a pilot named Chamberlin.

Lindbergh went back to St Louis to discuss the situation with his backers; there were at least four others in the race and they all had aircraft being prepared. The St Louis group agreed that he should keep on trying. The race was on.

On 23 February, he went to San Diego to meet the Ryan people. On the 25th, he made a down payment to them to close the deal and officially entered for the Orteig Prize the same day.

The Ryan factory on the waterfront at San Diego was a rather shabby place but the company turned out to be exactly the right one to build Charles Lindbergh's aircraft. The men there were his kind of people: tireless, dedicated and imaginative aeronautical enthusiasts who would do anything to give him what he wanted. It was a custom-built machine for one pilot, for one trip. The layout was based on a standard Ryan design but greatly modified to carry the huge fuel load. He agonised over every detail with the designer, Donald Hall, and the guiding principle was always how to reduce weight. Lindbergh wanted the cockpit behind the fuel tank, so that if he crashed, he would not be crushed between it and the engine. Consequently they had to abandon forward-facing windows and the pilot would be unable to see straight forward, and look out through little side windows.

That spring all the competitors were busy making their final preparations. In France, Nungesser was test-flying the PL8 which he had christened *L'Oiseau Blanc*. In New York, Levine was putting larger fuel tanks into the Wright/Bellanca and to squeeze every drop of publicity out of the press, he announced that an attempt would be made on the world endurance record when the aircraft was ready. Byrd was having modifications carried out to his Fokker in New Jersey and on 10 April Davis and his co-pilot Wooster flew to Langley Field, Virginia, for final test flights. The Lindbergh Ryan had yet to make its maiden flight.

The pace of events reached a crescendo.

On 13 April, Chamberlin broke the world endurance record in the Wright/Bellanca by staying aloft with his co-pilot, Bert Acosta, for over fifty-one hours, more than enough for the flight to Paris.

On 16 April, Commander Byrd's Fokker Trimotor, with the designer Anthony Fokker at the controls, crashed when landing after its maiden flight. Nobody was killed, but Byrd fractured his arm, and his pilot, Floyd Bennett, suffered a broken leg.

On 26 April Davis and Wooster were killed when the *American Legion* crashed on take-off for its final test flight at Langley, Virginia.

On 28 April Charles Lindbergh made his first test flight in the Ryan at San Diego. He was delighted with its performance but went carefully through a test programme, gradually building up the weight.

The field was narrowing: Nungesser, Chamberlin and now Lindbergh. Byrd's *America* was being repaired.

On 8 May, just as Lindbergh was carrying out the final tests on his aeroplane, news reached him that Nungesser and his navigator, Coli, had left Le Bourget in *L'Oiseau Blanc*. Next morning there was still no news of them and they were feared lost.

The weather on the Pacific coast held Lindbergh up for a few more precious days, but when it cleared on 10 May, Lindbergh set out for St Louis the same afternoon. While waiting for his aircraft to be built, Lindbergh had learned all he could about long-distance navigation especially over the sea and at night. The non-stop, 1550-mile night flight to St Louis, which was a record in itself, was intended as a practical test of both the aircraft and Lindbergh's skills. The aircraft's name – *The Spirit of St Louis* – was painted on the nose and the number, NX-211, across the top wing. The press began to take an interest and were out in force at Dutch Flats to see him off.

At 3.55 Pacific Time *The Spirit of St Louis* lifted off, escorted by aircraft from the Ryan Company and the local Naval Station. The escorts stayed with Lindbergh until he reached the mountains, then he was alone. Stretching ahead all he could see was the empty desert, parched and shimmering under the bright sun. As the sun gradually set behind him, the shadows on the ground lengthened and the valleys darkened. Soon, it started to get cold in the cockpit. Beyond the desert were higher mountains, barely visible in the gathering night. He climbed higher, into even colder air. Suddenly, the aircraft began to shake violently; the engine coughed and spluttered and began to lose power. Carburettor icing. It is a problem which every pilot dreads, especially over mountains, and he had a few moments of anxiety. He eased back the mixture control lever but the coughing went on. Slowly, slowly he began to lose altitude, closer and closer to the mountains. He scanned the dark slopes for a likely landing-spot but from several thousand feet up, he would have to wait until he was closer to see if the area was suitable. He opened the throttle full and eased it back again: the engine roared but it was still coughing, but gradually it began to run a little smoother. By manipulating the throttle and the mixture control until the vibration was least, he found that he could just coax the aircraft into a climb. The Rocky Mountains were ahead and he had to decide whether to try to go on, turn back, spiral over the spot until dawn or head south nearer the Mexican border where the mountains are lower and the air probably warmer. He chose to stick to the plan and climbed back into the cold air above the Rockies, juggling with throttle and mixture control and using a little more power than normal. He managed to scramble up to 13,000 feet and groped his way through the snow-capped mountain ridges which shone menacingly in the moonlight with just 500 feet clearance. He crossed the highest peaks just before midnight Pacific Time, about halfway to St Louis. As the mountains gave way to the plains of Oklahoma, he eased down to 8000 feet again and, free of icing, the engine ran smoothly. The stars began to fade and a rich orange glow seared along the black horizon as the first inkling of dawn came up ahead. In full daylight he scanned the ground below for landmarks to check his navigation. This had been his old stamping-ground in more boisterous times and he soon fixed his position. He was about fifty miles to the south of his track, but because of a brisk tailwind he was well ahead of time.

Once he knew where he was, it was a relatively simple flight to Lambert Field, St Louis, where a warm welcome from friends awaited him. The Robertson brothers were there, Harold Bixby, the broker who masterminded the financial support, and a host of others. Despite their obvious desire to keep him there, his friends and supporters all agreed that he should press on to New York the following day after a good rest, but first, after fourteen hours in the air, he was famished and went to his familiar breakfast joint – Louie's – for ham and eggs.

He flew to New York on 12 May and landed at Curtiss Field next to Roosevelt Field. The welcome was as enthusiastic as at Lambert, but the people were different: there were no friendly faces, just reporters, photographers and sightseers who swarmed round the aircraft, often in grave danger of being hit by the propeller. Once he was out of the cockpit the reporters and photographers crowded round.

The race to be first to fly the Atlantic flight was already big news and now Charles Lindbergh was really part of it. The reporters fired a barrage of questions at him, about the flight, about himself and about the other competitors. As they were grilling him, Commander Byrd's Fokker Trimotor landed.

The Wright/Bellanca was already there and scheduled to take off the following morning. Bert Acosta, the pilot who had broken the endurance record in it with Chamberlin, had pulled out of the team, exasperated with the wheeling and dealing of Levine. He was going to fly with Byrd instead. Levine had signed up another man called Bertaud. That night the weather closed in and put an end to speculation about the Wright/Bellanca taking off.

The weather kept everybody grounded for a week, but in the Levine camp there were other troubles brewing, generated by the inevitable clash of personalities and motives. The arguments about the division of spoils after the flight were raging even before it had been made. Bertaud was aggrieved to find that his contract gave Levine exclusive rights to his services for a year after the flight. They wrangled, had meetings with lawyers, sorted out a deal, then Levine went back on the deal. Finally a judge granted Bertaud an injunction, stopping the Wright/Bellanca from flying unless he was part of the crew.

Commander Byrd was not completely ready, and in any case, he saw the transatlantic flight more as a voyage of scientific discovery than a commercial enterprise. He was, moreover, a complete gentleman; he offered Lindbergh the use of his private runway at Roosevelt Field and the use of his weather reports. Lindbergh used the time to make final adjustments to his aircraft and he had a carburettor heater installed.

Newspaper interest rose to fever pitch that week; once, when Lindbergh was sitting in his hotel bedroom, two cameramen burst in, expecting to take photographs. They were swiftly ejected. Charles Lindbergh was already showing his distaste for such excesses of behaviour. He showed little of his resentment on the surface, he was too much in control for that, but inside he was angry. He simply could not understand how people could behave like that and made no concession to their style of behaviour. What he hated even more was the nicknames they gave him: 'Lindy' and 'Lucky Lindbergh'. When he went out to the airfield, spectators tried to touch him. It was bad enough when he was alone, but in the middle of it all, his mother arrived from Detroit. She was as cold and unresponsive as he was with the press: when they asked her to kiss him for the cameras she refused.

He couldn't wait to get away.

On the night of the 19th the weather was forecast to clear and after only a few hours of interrupted sleep he set out for the airfield. Neither Byrd nor Chamberlin was there; the former still had tests to run and the latter was still grounded by the injunction. So it was that Charles Lindbergh, the outsider in the race, who came from behind, a cool and unruffled figure in a world apparently gone mad with the superficial considerations, got to the starting-line first.

In the early morning, as *The Spirit of St Louis* skimmed over the lake at the end of the runway at Roosevelt Field, he was free at last from the crowds and the newspapermen who fed off their apparently insatiable appetite for garbage. But even when he was airborne they didn't leave him alone, for as he climbed away, aircraft appeared alongside with more photographers pressed up against the windows.

The flight was the greatest adventure he had ever embarked on. For a week he had been bottling up a tide of powerful emotions: excitement at the prospect of flying off alone, fear of crashing into the sea, determination to conquer those feelings, anger at the press, distaste for the crowds, anticipation of the weather reports and a competitive urge to beat the others. Adrenalin bubbled inside him but he kept it under control, hiding everything from those around him, save the occasional flash of temper with photographers. These tensions, coupled with the detailed work of making the final plans for the flight, meant that he had hardly slept for days.

As he flew along the East Coast towards his last landfall over Newfoundland, the effects of the last few days in New York began to tell and drowsiness began to overtake him. Sitting in the cockpit, alone, and surrounded by the hypnotic drone of the engine, his only real tasks were to physically control the aircraft and to navigate. The flight very quickly became a constant struggle against sleepiness. His tense and exhausted body was constantly sending signals to the brain that it needed rest, but between mind and body lay Lindbergh's iron determination. He sipped water from his canteen, he scooped air from the slipstream through the window on to his face and forced himself to concentrate on the instruments and the navigation.

Over St John's, Newfoundland, he eased slightly off course to fly low over the town, a farewell gesture which was immediately picked up by America's press and relayed round the world. It was a gripping moment for the millions who were following his progress. Their hero was, at that very moment, setting out alone into the emptiness of the Atlantic which only a week ago had claimed the lives of Nungesser and Coli on the same mission.

Slowly, slowly, the coast of Canada slipped out of sight behind, and the sky ahead began to darken as night fell over the ocean. The last twinkling lights faded and stars appeared overhead in a darkening, crystal sky. Below, wreathed in swirling fog, icebergs, the ghostly natives of the Atlantic, loomed under the wing. Soon it was dark and he was completely alone. The cockpit became his home, a warm and friendly place in a cold and hostile world. The luminous dials of the instruments stared at him cosily, communicating gently all the information he needed about the world outside. On his knee a map showed him the vastness of his enterprise; next to it was his log which spelt it out in neat figures. The note of the engine was smooth, reassuring and soporific.

Outside, the mood of the Atlantic was changing. Ahead, his path was blocked by huge columns of cloud which rose higher than he could see. He held his course and disciplined his mind for instrument flying, eyes darting from one dial to the next as *The Spirit of St Louis* flew into the milky whiteness. Inside it was like flying through a subterranean vault carved out of cloud; sometimes he was in the clear spaces, sometimes he had to fly through the clouds themselves and they buffeted him remorselessly. Ice began to form on the aircraft and the tubes which fed information to the instruments were slowly becoming encrusted. It could be a fatal problem: to test the air, Lindbergh put his arm out of the window and felt the prickly stinging of ice crystals against his skin. He took out his flashlight and shone it along the wing-struts and saw irregular-shaped growths forming on the aircraft. It was time to get out of the cloud. He groped his way between the thick, grey pillars, always heading south towards the shipping lanes. The professional pilot in him said 'Turn back'; the adventurer in him said 'Go on'. The adventurer won.

Gradually the gaps between the clouds became bigger than the clouds themselves; soon he was flying down valleys flanked by a rolling, fluffy landscape towards the dawn. With dawn came an overwhelming tiredness. The engine droned on and on, and the newly risen sun sparkled over the lonely horizon, probing into the cockpit from dead ahead, straight into his eyes. He tried everything to stay awake, diving the aircraft, sticking his head out of the window, but it was no good. He started daydreaming. Several times he fell asleep only to be woken as the aircraft immediately went into a diving turn, jolting him awake. Hour after hour he fought his body for control of its actions: dozing, concentrating on the compass, dozing again, dropping into sleep, then, almost immediately, the rude awakening.

The first signs of life over the ocean were gulls. Then, almost unbelievably, there was a fishing fleet rolling about in the waves. He was desperate for company and the prospect of seeing fellow human beings made him alert again. He dived down and examined the boats, but they were deserted. Was it at mirage? No, a head came out through a porthole and peered up at him. No wave, no recognition. He throttled back and shouted, asking the way to Ireland.

The face stared back expressionless. Keen as he was to communicate with somebody, he realised that boats could not be far from land and so, reluctantly, left the fishermen to their Saturday afternoon chores and flew on east. Sure enough, peering through rain squalls, he saw the horizon begin to harden and gradually it turned into a coastline.

It was Dingle Bay, Ireland: he was only fractionally off course and well ahead of time. He knew the wind had been behind him all the way but it had been stronger than he thought. He was over-joyed. He took stock of his situation: there was plenty of fuel and from here to Paris should be easy. He was alert now, exhilarated, he had done it. The excitement dredged up the last reserves of strength in his body.

He flew over Ireland, Cornwall and the Channel. He ate a sandwich, his first food for a day and a half. Over the coast of France at last; the Orteig Prize was his now for the rules stipulated that the flight had only to reach France to qualify.

The news that he had made it across the Atlantic was immediately flashed round the world. Paris erupted in a wave of emotion and Parisians set off for Le Bourget airfield in their thousands. Alone and high over the French countryside as dusk fell on a quiet Saturday, his second evening without a break from the cockpit, Lindbergh was unaware of the reception which was building up. He was more concerned with finding Paris. Paris was lit up like a Christmas tree and with the Eiffel Tower as a landmark he had little difficulty in finding Le Bourget. As he flew over, he could see the floodlit concrete apron, the hangars, and around them a mass of bobbing lights, like fireflies. He aimed for the dark patch in front of the hangars and glided down to land and began to turn, to taxi instinctively towards the hangars. Suddenly he was aware of running figures all around the aircraft. He cut the engine and was immediately surrounded by excited people, their faces pressed up against the windows, their voices chanting: 'Lindbergh, Lindbergh.'

He heard a snap, then another, then another. He heard a ripping sound as the fabric, the very skin of his beloved *Spirit of St Louis*, was torn off by souvenir-hunters. When he got out of the cockpit to try to find a guard for his aircraft, his feet barely touched French soil before he was carried aloft into the crowd.

His reception in Paris was one long tumult of extravagant celebration: wherever he went in public he was mobbed by crowds of screaming fans and he was presented with gold medals and citations. In private, he was received into the most exclusive society drawing-rooms, the ultimate catch for every host and hostess. It was the same in London. At Buckingham Palace, King George V asked him privately: 'How did you pee?'

Instant stardom hardly ruffled his manner, he appeared to take it all in his stride, and so steadfast was his boyish nature in the face of such an onslaught of adulation that it fuelled the adulation all the more. In a flighty and superficial age he shone like a beacon of purity: a flashing smile, handsome, clean-cut, sober, well-mannered, single, at ease with one and all, though stirringly shy with girls.

He planned to go back to America the long way round, flying *The Spirit of St Louis* right round the world, but the President of the United States had other ideas and saw to it that he came home to give the American public a chance to lionise him before the clamour died down. The USS *Memphis* docked at Cherbourg to take him home. He sailed up the Potomac in style; America was welcoming its hero as only America could and as they had never done before: wave after wave of aircraft flew overhead as the hero sailed home, armadas of little ships criss-crossed the river, sirens sounded, factory whistles shrieked, church bells rang and crowds and crowds of people blocked every approach to the dock where the *Memphis* tied up. Fifteen guns were fired in honour of the admiral; twenty-one in honour of Lindbergh. Nothing was too good for him. The admiral went ashore and escorted Lindbergh's mother on board to greet America's son. Tears trickled on thousands of cheeks as mother and son were reunited, dry-eyed.

They appeared on a platform with President Coolidge and dined with the Cabinet. He was formally presented with the Orteig Prize – a cheque for $25,000. Invitations, business propositions and marriage proposals poured in from all over the country. The souvenir industry wound itself up into a frenzied orgy of entrepreneurial tastelessness: songs were written and poetry composed; commemorative *objets d'art* were sold in their thousands, china, glassware, lapel badges, shoes, embroidery . . .

Throughout it all Charles Lindbergh retained not only his healthy, clean-cut image, but he kept his wits about him too. He was clearly going to be rich but he restricted the business propositions to the furtherance of commercial aviation; he stuck to his original goal. The Guggenheim Fund and the US Department of Commerce sponsored a tour for him to demonstrate that commercial aviation was practical, punctual and safe. If the tour achieved its purpose, few cared; its function was lost in the outpouring of emotion towards Lindbergh himself; it simply fuelled the inferno of his popularity to a new intensity. Conventional wisdom said that it would die down, but as the weeks and months went by it not only endured, it grew and grew. Lindbergh – consciously or unconsciously is debatable – appeared reluctant, modest, an ordinary guy. People could identify with him and they did in their millions; his wholesomeness shone through the murky web of politics, business and slick promotion.

There was, too, a romantic dimension to his image; he was single, handsome and extremely attractive to women and yet he was uncomfortably shy and squirmed at the many advances which were made. The whole media circus and the depths to which it induced people to go – reaching out to touch him, screaming at the sight of him, calling his name, stealing his belongings – disgusted him. His life up to then had been spent either alone, with his mother, or in the small, close-knit and very narrow world of aviation. When confronted with the excesses of America-at-large, he was genuinely horrified by them.

By October 1927, he had flown over 20,000 miles across America and given speeches which he confined to commercial aviation. He ignored questions about his private life. But the less he said, the more the press wanted, the more he loathed them, the less he said, and so on, ad infinitum.

His popularity was not confined to the masses; the rich and powerful wanted his company too and they offered him something he wanted badly – privacy. Gradually but inexorably he was driven into the company of bankers and businessmen. Harry Guggenheim, whose fund had financed his trip around America, invited him to make his home on his palatial estate on the shores of Long Island. There, he had hundreds of acres to roam in, a private airstrip, private beach and discreet servants.

In December 1927 he was invited by the US Ambassador to Mexico, Dwight Morrow, to fly to Mexico City. His trip to Paris had done wonders for Franco-American relations and the ambassador was anxious to repeat the performance with America's southern, and sometimes trying, neighbour. As a diplomatic instrument, Lindbergh was a great success and the flight did indeed improve relations. More importantly for Lindbergh, the ambassador invited him and his mother to stay for Christmas and subsequently he became an intimate friend of the Morrow family.

The ambassador was not the only one who saw his potential as an adornment. In June 1928, he was invited by Transcontinental Air Transport to become chairman of their technical committee, a post he gladly accepted for it meant he could do a worthwhile job in commercial aviation, flying route-proving flights. He tried to slide out of the public eye, but it didn't work. He tried to keep the details of his flights secret to avoid crowds gathering at his destinations, but it didn't work. Once after leaving Tampico, Mexico, after a visit to the Morrow family he was expected to fly to Brownsville, Texas. He didn't; he landed elsewhere and set off wild speculation in the press that he had crashed. Whatever he did was news and he had no control over which of his actions was reported and which was not and it irked him greatly. But there is an irony about his attitude towards the press and publicity, for though he professed a great antipathy for the attention they gave him, he did little to avoid fuelling it. However naïve he was (or pretended to be), when he led the Army Air Corps flying team at air displays, stunting and pulling all the old barnstorming tricks out of the bag to thrill the crowds, he could hardly have believed that it was not going to be sensational material for the newspapers. Equally, when he disappeared from view afterwards, he knew that it only made the public and the press hounds all the keener. He never quite managed to step out of the limelight completely, instead, he stayed in it, and confronted those whom he protested he wanted to avoid.

On 12 February 1929, he married Ambassador Morrow's daughter, Anne. Anne Morrow was a highly educated woman but not of the same scientific inclination as Lindbergh. Her interests were the arts, literature, poetry. So secret were the arrangements for the wedding that even the guests, who were family friends, only knew they were going to a wedding at the last moment. Afterwards, the couple were smuggled away for a honeymoon sailing off the Atlantic coast. The press eventually found them and pestered them.

It was not a society wedding, nor was it a society marriage. She had to learn the tools of his trade: navigation, aircraft maintenance, Morse code, radio operation. She took her gliding licence and Lindbergh taught her to fly. They led a very full existence together but it was based firmly on aviation and followed his dynamic path through life.

In June 1930 their first baby was born – a son who was named after his father.

The press pestered them for pictures and Lindbergh's relations with them reached a new low. But this hounding by the press, and the quite extraordinary popular desire for details of their lives, was to reach much greater and more tragic depths. Early in 1932 the Lindbergh family moved into a new house they had built on an isolated 400-acre site in the Sourland Mountains. Anne was pregnant again. Very soon afterwards, their son was kidnapped, taken from his cot while he was asleep. A ladder was found against the house. A ransom note arrived asking for $50,000 for the safe return of the child. The greatest pain, the greatest tragedy any parents could suffer was, at the same time, instantly the biggest human interest news-story since Lindbergh's transatlantic flight. Every newspaper wanted coverage and they sent teams of reporters; circulation rose; the public held its breath as the story developed, as every lead (some real but mostly bogus) was given banner headlines. Publicity-seekers jumped on the bandwagon: film stars, private individuals tried to attach themselves to the search by coming up with spurious leads, just to be associated with the Lindberghs. Even Al Capone, from his prison cell, offered to help.

A ransom was paid through an intermediary but there was no sign of the baby. The Lindberghs feared the worst but continued to hope. Charles Lindbergh, clutching at straws, was convinced by the sincerity of one man, called Curtis, who said he knew who was holding the baby and could arrange a rendezvous at sea. He kept up the pretence for weeks, going out in a boat with Lindbergh. Then the news came that the baby's body had been found and Lindbergh realised that Curtis was just another publicity-seeker. Press photographers tried to break into the morgue for a photograph of the body.

There was widespread sympathy for the Lindberghs after the death of their son but the thousands of letters, the sightseers who came to look at the house where the baby had lived, only further dispirited and disgusted the Lindberghs. Anne had her second child in August the same year and family life of a sort went on, but Charles Lindbergh was obsessed with finding the kidnapper.

There was little he could do practically and while the search for the killer went on he continued with his work for the airlines. In the spring of 1933, he took Anne with him on a long survey flight for Pan American Airways over the North Atlantic, across Europe, down to West Africa, across the South Atlantic to Brazil and back to New York via the Caribbean. But his work was not limited to flying for the airlines and advising them on routes; when they came under attack from the government, he took up the political cudgels for them too.

In February 1934, President Roosevelt's New Deal, his crusade on behalf of the small man and the casualties of the Depression and against the vested interests of big business, was in the full bloom of its novelty and idealism. In this context, the airlines were now big business and a large part of their revenue came from contracts to carry the US Mail. There was evidence of irregularities in the way the contracts had been bid for and awarded, there were close relationships between some officials and representatives of the airlines and the companies were making huge profits. Lindbergh had a particular fondness for the airmail business for he had started his career there and when the President cancelled the contracts and brought in the Army to do the job, Lindbergh saw it as an attack on the whole airline industry, declaring them all guilty for the possible crimes of a few, and that without any trial. For the President it was part of his overall plan to clean up business; for Lindbergh it was a simple miscarriage of justice and the two views, coming from two such different people, were irreconcilable. They were diametrically opposed: the President was a 'man of the people', the masses; Lindbergh was his own man, but he was now, unmistakably, aligned with the rich and powerful. Lindbergh sent a telegram to the President and a copy to the press at the same time (the press were not so low that they could not be used when it suited) and the issue became obscured in the battle between the personalities. It soon became evident that Army pilots could not do the job properly and, as Lindbergh had foretold, pilots began to be killed. The public duel between Roosevelt and Lindbergh, the wrangling over issues through personalities, went on for some months and in the end, the airlines got their contracts back, but at much reduced cost to the Post Office and after a clean-up in the way the contracts were awarded. Neither party really won the duel, but it was the beginning of a relationship of mutual distaste between Lindbergh and Roosevelt which was to last for a long time.

Lindbergh was still in demand as a pilot, and in August 1934, he flew Pan American's giant new Sikorsky Clipper from Bridgeport, Connecticut, to Brazil in eight hours, breaking all records and further establishing America as an international civil air power. He formed a close relationship with Juan Trippe, the equally dynamic founder and architect of the worldwide network of routes which Pan American Airways established.

A month after that flight, the police arrested a German immigrant called Hauptmann for the murder of the Lindberghs' baby and the press bandwagon, never far away, began to roll again with a new intensity. Photographers began pestering their new baby, Jon, on his way to school, trying to snatch photographs and once forcing the car he was travelling in to stop. It seemed impossible to get the press to give up. The trial lasted six weeks and on 13 February 1935, Hauptmann was found guilty and sentenced to death. The trial and the publicity surrounding it combined into a bizarre theatre that provoked an outpouring of sympathy for the Number One American hero. Hauptmann stood little chance as America purged itself for its treatment of the Lindberghs.

After the appeals procedure had been exhausted, Hauptmann finally went to the electric chair on 3 April 1936. The Lindberghs were not in America to witness it; in December 1935, the family had set up home in England. They had had enough of America.

In England Lindbergh was just as much a hero as in America but the English treated their heroes, and other people's, rather differently than the Americans and it was a way which was much more to the Lindberghs' taste. America agonised over their departure and Americans rebuked themselves roundly for the appalling harassment which they had suffered and which, with hindsight, few Americans could deny had driven their hero away. After an initial flurry of interest and a brief surge when the man convicted of the baby's murder went to the electric chair, the British press left the Lindberghs politely alone.

By comparison with America, their new surroundings were idyllic. They rented Long Barn at Weald in Kent. It belonged to Harold Nicolson and his wife Vita Sackville-West who lived close by in Sissinghurst. The contrast in lifestyle was therapeutic for the whole family: shopping in the village shop, walks in the lanes of 'the Garden of England', the casual conversation with some of the most stimulating minds in the country.

It was not entirely a life of rural bliss, Lindbergh was too active a man for that. He was still in demand as a dinner guest in the houses of the great and good and dined with the new King Edward and his future wife, the then Mrs Wallis Simpson, shortly after he ascended the throne. But Lindbergh was always on the look-out for a new challenge, for more exciting pursuits, and when the US diplomatic service sought him out for an unusual assignment, he responded with enthusiasm.

The military attaché in Berlin, Major Truman, invited him to come to Germany to tour the German aircraft industry and make an appraisal of both civil and military developments. The letter of invitation made it quite clear that it was sent at the instigation of the German Air Minister and General of the Luftwaffe, Hermann Goering. Lindbergh could see whatever he wanted to and since the press in Germany was controlled, he could choose what was reported and what was not. The attaché clearly wanted him to come and hinted that it would be very interesting for the US Government to have his appreciation of the German air capability.

It was an invitation he could hardly refuse and from everybody's point of view the trip was a great success. Lindbergh enjoyed his tour of such an advanced and burgeoning aircraft industry, the attaché had the benefit of his observations and the National Socialist Government of Germany was able not only to parade their aircraft before a distinguished and influential visitor, but their policies for a revitalised Germany as well. Lindbergh went back to England deeply impressed with both aspects of Germany. In the National Socialist Movement he saw the answer to so many of the ills he perceived in his own country and in 'decadent' Britain, and in the powerful German air force he saw something which could be used by that movement to devastating effect. That was precisely the impression which the German Government intended, though they could hardly have imagined that Lindbergh would use his observations to such effect on their behalf. In American terms he was politically naïve, but in the labyrinthine ways of European politics he was a complete innocent.

From his brief impression of the German nation and its air force he set out to convince anybody who would listen that Germany should be both accommodated and feared. He made further visits to Germany and reinforced his views in discussions with Goering, Milch and Udet, the architects of German air power, and was duped into thinking that the Luftwaffe was much more powerful than it really was. Germany stimulated him: he was awarded Germany's highest award for bravery in the air; he met Willy Messerschmitt. These visits gave him a new purpose.

He went back to America determined to stop war, if possible, and to keep his country out of it if it did happen. When war came, once again he found himself opposing the President root and branch. Roosevelt's policy was to help Britain to the limits of America's status as a neutral country. In reality, with programmes such as Lend-Lease, he turned America into Britain's bankers and Britain's arsenal. Lindbergh was passionate in his opposition, not only to the possibility of direct American involvement in the war but also to America supporting Britain. He took every suitable platform to speak: he addressed thousands of America First rallies, he gave talks on the radio and testified before the House Foreign Affairs Committee against Lend-Lease. He was not alone in his drive to keep America out of the war, there was a substantial body of opinion in America which agreed with him. He was not the instigator of the movement, he became a figurehead.

For the hotchpotch of more astute political minds in the America First Committee he was a tremendous asset.

Opinion was split in America but the ground swell was behind the President; possibly not for outright war, but certainly for providing help to Britain. Lindbergh was a persistent thorn in the President's side rather than a substantial threat to his policies, but he was a prominent figure actively campaigning against the President and the President pulled no punches in seeking to diminish his effectiveness. In an interview, he more than hinted that the reason that Lindbergh had not been called up for duty as a reserve officer in the Air Corps was because men with his defeatist views were not wanted in the service. This thinly veiled attack on his patriotism stung Lindbergh. His response was petulance disguised as high principle; he resigned his reserve commission in the Air Corps.

As the mood of America slowly, but inexorably, came more and more behind the President, so Lindbergh was more and more implacably opposed to him and his policies. Secretly, his patriotism was called into more serious question; he was put under surveillance by the FBI and his telephone was tapped.

There were racial undertones in Lindbergh's anti-war stance; he wanted an alliance of peoples of European descent, including Germans, to oppose what he saw as a communist, but more particularly Asian, threat. And in the end it was sentiments such as these which accelerated the decline in his popularity. In a speech at Des Moines, he warned Jews in America against what he saw as their pro-war stance and against using their ownership and influence in the motion-picture business, the radio, press and government, to persuade people in that direction.

After that his personal popularity, which had always been his only real platform, declined sharply.

He was already separated from the Morrow family through difference of opinion; they preferred not to see him. Many of his friends from happier times also avoided him and some spoke out against him, but his implacable opposition to Roosevelt and his policies never wavered and on the eve of the Japanese attack on Pearl Harbor he was still planning speeches.

Once America was at war, he stopped speaking, but Roosevelt then denied him the one means by which he could rehabilitate his reputation. He was turned down for service in the Air Corps in a personal interview with the Secretary of War, Henry Stimson. With his skills as an engineer and aviator, and driven by never-flagging dynamism, he would have been an asset in any part of the aircraft industry, but he was on the wrong side of a new mood in America and even getting a worthwhile war job was difficult. He was eventually employed by the right-wing industrialist, Henry Ford, at the Willow Run bomber plant.

Later in the war he managed to get into combat. He went to the Pacific ostensibly on a tour as an aviation consultant but through his standing among pilots for his skill, he managed to include combat missions on his itinerary.

The views he expressed in the late 1930s dogged him for the rest of his life. After the war, he wrote the definitive account of his transatlantic flight, called *The Spirit of St Louis*, and he was still in demand as an aviation consultant. He was gradually rehabilitated into the American pantheon of heroes but his reputation was always simmering in the controversy of his stance before the war and it occasionally boiled over into nasty disputes. He died in 1974.

He was, without doubt, one of the great achievers in aviation and one of the great popular heroes of this century. His contribution to the progress of civil aviation in particular is immense, both technically and through his promotion of its interests. Whatever the endeavour, straightforward or complex, flying the Atlantic single-handed or keeping America out of a war, he applied himself to it totally and often, with the more complex matters, narrowly. His successes were the product of dynamism and purposefulness; his failures the product of that same dynamism stunted by a lack of real vision. He wove a web around his achievements in which he himself became entangled.

8 Charles Yeager

There was little to distinguish Hamlin from the thousands of other small towns in rural America. The address was Lincoln County, West Virginia. Population: 1200. Hamlin served a community of small farmers and businessmen: there were lawyers, shops, merchants, a host of churches, a school, and a pool hall. Hamlin was Small Town America writ large on the landscape.

Charles Yeager was born in Hamlin in 1923. His father was a gas driller, prospecting for pockets of natural gas in the coalfields. He was away from the family a great deal, so Charles, his elder brother Roy and sister Pearl were bought up mainly by their mother. At home, the family routine was built around subsistence farming: cows to milk, chickens to feed, garden to work, barn to fix, grace at mealtimes and Bible classes every Sunday.

At high school he just coasted. He loved football, games, playing the trombone and marching with the band. Outside school and farm chores, he read Mark Twain and Jack London and wandered in the Appalachian Mountains, learning to hunt, shoot and fish from an early age. It was an idyllic life in some ways but Hamlin offered little in the way of fresh opportunity. Roy became a gas driller like his father and when Charles left school, he cleaned the town photographer's studio and later worked in the pool hall.

In the summer of 1941 army recruiting sergeants came to Hamlin. There was a war raging in faraway Europe and though America was still neutral, the Army was looking for recruits. Charles Yeager liked the style of the sergeant who was doing his bit for the Air Corps. He offered Yeager an ambition, to become a pilot. Yeager spoke to his father about it, who said they would probably draft him anyway, so on 12 September 1941 Charles went into Huntington with his father and enlisted.

There was a long way to go before he could learn to fly. To become a cadet and join as a student pilot, a young man needed a college education. There were opportunities for enlisted men without college, but it was a longer and a tougher route. Charles Yeager had no college education so his first experience of the Army was the short sharp shock of basic GI training: up early in the mornings for drill and PT. After a rather brutal induction into the Army he was trained as a mechanic and was soon on his first job with aeroplanes as crew chief on P-6 fighters at Moppet Field in California. His job was to look after the aircraft on the ground, service the engine and care for it when it was not flying. He had to learn to taxi it on the ground. It was a great way to learn about aircraft and he learned quickly, tinkering with the various systems, finding out not only how they worked but what they did and why. On 4 December 1941, just three days before America came into the war, he applied for training as a pilot.

But he had to wait. In 1942, he was posted to Victorville to work on twin-engined AT-11s which were used to train bomber crews, and it was in an AT-11 that he got his first chance to fly. It was not a very auspicious occasion; the engineering officer took him for a flight which, as a passenger, he did not find at all exciting and in no time at all he was violently sick.

That summer he was called up for flying training. There were other enlisted men on the course but they were outnumbered five to one by cadets, men with college education who were destined to become officers, and they were all housed and trained together. Before they started flying they had to go to ground school: lessons in aircraft systems, how they worked, the principles of flight, engines, airframes. Yeager had been working on aircraft for nearly a year by then and he knew a lot about them. He was sure of himself; he knew more than many of the cadets and as far as he was concerned, enlisted man or officer, he was as good as anybody. His self-confidence had an effect on his general attitude and with his permanent grin and smiling eyes he appeared cocky and was cautioned several times to change or be 'washed out'. He toned down, but it was difficult to hide his bursting self-assurance and enthusiasm.

It was not just his face which showed it, his whole approach to life in the Air Corps was positive, he was eager to learn and impatient to do things. He was only an average pilot in training, but he loved the lifestyle: it was busy and it was competitive; he would show those cadets that he was as good as any of them, and better. As flying training became steadily more and more intensive, his eagerness and self-confidence grew with it.

Most military pilots in training want to be fighter pilots, to follow the heritage of McCudden, Richthofen, and the American aces, Eddie Rickenbacker and Frank Luke. A fighter pilot fights on his own, he needs to be self-assured and aggressive, and he needs to relish the opportunities to fly aircraft to their known limits and beyond. The pushiness, the cockiness, the eagerness, though controlled by his instructors on the one hand, was, they knew, exactly what was needed in a fighter squadron and when Chuck Yeager was awarded his wings, he was posted to the 357th Fighter Group at Tonopah, Nevada, to fly the P-39 Bell Airacobra fighter.

It was the summer of 1943; his squadron was preparing for war. The pilots were going through a most intensive training period, flying a hundred hours a month – dogfighting, dive-bombing, skip-bombing and ground-strafing. It was a perfect environment for Yeager: he was twenty, he was flying and there was more than enough to do. He liked the lifestyle, living closely with other men of his own age and character who had been through the same training. As they flew, trained and played together, they became a tightly-knit group, they knew each other's flying habits and could work instinctively together in the air. He was still a GI, he was a flight officer which was an appointment, not a commission, but in the squadron what mattered was what a pilot could do in the air and what his overall attitude was. Yeager fitted in well.

One day he was leading a flight at 18,000 feet when he saw a bomber far below at 5000 feet. Never missing an opportunity to indulge in mock combat and to show his flare as a fighter pilot, he told the flight to follow and went into a screaming dive. They flew head-on at the bomber in turn to frighten the crew before passing above or below. After his pass, Yeager continued to dive for the ground, going flat out as always. Suddenly, there was a loud explosion just behind him; smoke filled the cockpit and one of the doors was blown off. The engine was just behind the pilot in the P-39 and it was on fire. He managed to roll through the door and tumble out but he was upside down as he pulled the ripcord and when the parachute jerked him upright, the blow knocked him unconscious. He woke up in hospital.

In a month he was fit to fly again and sailed with his squadron to Britain and to war. His confidence, and the squadron's, was at a peak. They knew what they could do, they had tangled with each other in dogfights time and time again in the blue skies over Nevada, but the ultimate test was combat and Yeager was impatient to do some real fighting. It was all very well dogfighting with your buddies, but what it led to, the reason Chuck Yeager had been put on earth and given an aeroplane, was to get into combat.

Sailing up the Clyde to dock at Greenock was a depressing entry into the war. It was a bitterly cold day and the sky was overcast with a soapy mixture of cloud and industrial smog. On the dock a band tried to coax a tune out of frozen instruments.

His squadron was to be re-equipped with America's latest and deadliest fighter, the P-51 Mustang. Their task would be to escort bombers on the long flights into Germany and protect them from the Luftwaffe. Until the Mustangs arrived they had to wait and live in Nissen huts on the hurriedly-built airfields in East Anglia in winter. It was cruel to eager young fighter pilots from sunny Nevada. Unlike the other squadrons, they were idle, but when their P-51s did arrive in late January 1944, they were worth waiting for: powerful, fast and well-armed, they were a pilot's aeroplane. Yeager had the name – *Glamorous Glennis* – painted on the nose; Glennis was his girlfriend. He was ready for combat.

The target for his first combat mission was Hamburg. This was the moment he had been training for, he was going to tangle with the enemy. It was a huge operation: forming up with the bombers, heading out over the North Sea, always keeping a wary eye out for German fighters. Here and there he got a glimpse of the German countryside, he saw the bomb strikes, a bit of flak but no fighters. When they turned for home and he had not fired a shot, it was an anticlimax. The next few missions were the same. Once they saw some German aircraft, but their orders were to protect the bombers, not to leave them open to a trap. He was learning, but he still yearned for that ultimate competition between pilots – aerial combat.

On 4 March 1944 he escorted bombers on one of the first daylight raids on Berlin. The weather was cloudy and he lost most of the squadron and over Germany he was with just one other pilot, high above the bomber stream, when the Germans attacked. Yeager saw an Me-109 alone in the sky: it was the answer to his prayers, a lone German to shoot at. He dived at full power for the Me-109 which grew bigger in his sights; suddenly he realised that in his eagerness for a fight, he was going far too fast, he was going to miss the shot. He pulled back the power and aileron-rolled, violently killing off the excess speed, then slid in below and behind the 109. It just sat there. Yeager lined up quickly and fired: pieces flew off the Messerschmitt, it caught fire and the pilot baled out.

He had faced the ultimate test and passed; it was good to score; he was blooded. Yet Yeager was somehow disappointed: the German pilot didn't do anything, he had just sat there and got shot down. All the eagerness and enthusiasm had built up so much that the reality seemed once again an anticlimax.

The next day, Yeager was shot down. The squadron was escorting bombers to Bordeaux. Not far from the target they were jumped by some Focke-Wulf-190s and as soon as Yeager saw them, he turned to meet them head-on and instantly became a target himself; 20-mm cannon shells started slamming into his Mustang with sickening accuracy; the propeller flew to pieces in front of his face; the oxygen system exploded and a big hole appeared in one wing; shell splinters seared into both his feet. His Mustang was falling; he baled out at about 17,000 feet, free-falling to about 5000 feet.

He was lucky. He landed among some saplings and not long after he had stowed his parachute, a woman appeared and indicated for him to follow her. Within a few minutes he was buried in the hay in a barn and when the Germans came, they searched the barn, but they missed him. He stayed there for hours before the woman came back and took him into the house to tend to his wounds. He stayed at the farm for a few days, then an agent from the Maquis came with bicycles and he cycled away in a suit of the farmer's clothes. He was passed along a chain of contacts towards the Spanish border. Just before he reached the border, he was joined by three other American pilots who were in a similar position. Their guide took them up into the Pyrenees, then left them just short of the border after explaining where to cross. The four Americans set off up the snow-covered road, then a shot rang out and the third man, Patterson, fell wounded in the knee. The other two were ahead. Yeager raced up to him and dragged him off the road to hide. That night he dragged Patterson over the mountains, evading the Germans, then down the other side where they were both arrested by Spanish guards and put in jail. After two lazy months in Spain while the US and Spanish authorities sorted out his case, he was flown back to England from Gibraltar on 3 June 1944.

He was anxious to get back into combat and he said so while he was being debriefed by the security specialists. But there was a policy that all those who had evaded capture with the help of the Resistance had to go back to the United States so that their contacts in France would not be compromised. Yeager refused to accept the policy. When the staff officer told him he was as good as on the next ship to New York, he demanded to see the next officer up the ladder. Next day, he saw the deputy of Operations, a brigadier-general, and put the same case; he wanted to get back into combat and he wanted to go back to his squadron, that was where he belonged.

At nine o'clock the following morning he was standing in front of the Supreme Allied Commander, General Eisenhower. He put his case again, with all the pushiness which the difference in their relative status would allow. Even though he was Supreme Allied Commander, Eisenhower could not change the policy, but he was obviously impressed by Yeager's eagerness for combat and said he would ask permission from Washington to decide who did and who did not fly on combat missions. What he did not explain to Yeager was that the invasion was about to start and that the point about compromising French contacts would have less importance.

While waiting for a decision from Washington, Chuck was sent back to his squadron to start flying, but strictly at home. Yeager lived and breathed fighter tactics and on the squadron he taught new pilots all he could, taking them up and dogfighting with them. But real combat was what he wanted, he felt his whole existence depended on getting back into the fight. Six weeks later, authority came through for Eisenhower to decide and Yeager went back into the fight.

He was still a flight officer, a GI, an enlisted man; but his personality and skill as a fighter pilot made him a useful leader in the air and in 1944, over Germany, that is what counted. He never thought of the outcome of a fight – the most important thing was to fight and survive. Nothing was predictable; a fighter pilot had to cope with the realities of combat as they occurred; flying in combat meant getting into the unpredictable, the unknown, and finding a way out. Late 1944 was the best time of his life; it was the lifestyle, the rugged and dynamic existence, the fighting and the comradeship of the squadron. He loved it.

Sometimes he led the whole group of three squadrons. On 12 October he was leading the group at 28,000 feet, once again escorting bombers, when a formation of twenty-two Me-109s flew right across their path at the same level. He dropped the Mustang's extra fuel tanks in preparation for a fight. He manoeuvred the squadron with the sun behind them into a good position at 1000 yards, then closed to 600 yards and opened fire.

For the next few minutes the sky was full of twisting and turning aircraft; confusion reigned at 300 or 400 miles an hour. In the middle of it all, cool as ever, was Yeager, picking his targets, cranking the Mustang into the tightest turns and firing just at the right moment. He was vividly aware of everything going on around him and anticipated his moves; he was at his coolest when there was much to do and in that single fight he shot down five 109s while the rest of the squadron managed another two.

For that battle he was awarded the Silver Star, vindicating Eisenhower's decision to keep him in Europe. He was clearly an expert at his job but the had no particular ambition to become an officer. He lived life from day to day, doing his job and thirsting for combat. But he did not remain a non-com for long and when promotion came, it came in a rush: he rose from second lieutenant to captain in about two months.

That winter the Luftwaffe fielded its latest aircraft, the Me-262, a twin-engined jet fighter which was faster even than the Mustang. On 6 November Yeager was leading a section over Germany when the squadron leader saw three 262s out to the right. The whole squadron peeled over towards them and Yeager's section was then in the lead. When the Mustangs opened fire, the jets just used their greater speed to pull away. No sooner had they lost one flight of jets when they met another, head-on. Yeager fired at the leader and the German formation broke up, but even though he managed to get behind, fire and see strikes, the jet once again simply put on power and pulled away with ease. Yeager lost the squadron in the fight so he climbed back up to 8000 feet and headed north. He flew over a German airfield at just the right moment. A jet, a 262, was coming in to land low and slow. He put the Mustang into a power dive and raced round at 500 mph to attack the vulnerable German aircraft. Ground gunners opened up as he flew round the airfield boundary and as they found his range, the flak began to thicken up. He opened fire at 400 yards; he saw strikes on the 262's wings, then pulled back on the stick, converting speed into height to escape the ground fire. As he climbed, he saw the 262 crash into a wood just short of the runway.

Shooting down a jet from a propeller-driven aircraft was quite an achievement, even if it was coming in to land at the time, and Yeager was awarded the Distinguished Flying Cross. He was living proof that, however advanced the machinery of war became, it was the human element which counted in combat. He had been in Europe just a year; he was twenty-two years old; he had flown 64 combat sorties totalling 270 combat hours; he had shot down 11 enemy aircraft and damaged several more; he had been shot down and evaded, he had been commissioned and his officer's uniform had several rows of medals, most of them for individual acts of bravery and flying skill. It was January 1945: the war in Europe was coming to a close and with complete superiority in the air, Allied pilots found less and less opportunity for combat. It was the end of his tour and time to go home. Back in America, he married

Glennis whose name had gone into combat with him on the Mustang's nose. They went back to Hamlin together and the town turned out for its war hero and paraded him in the streets.

It had been a busy time, but it was only a year and he still had the whole of his life ahead of him. He could have flown for the airlines or found some other life but he loved being in the Air Force. Evaders and POWs were able to select which base they served at after the war and Yeager chose Wright-Patterson Field near Dayton, Ohio, principally because it was close to Hamlin. But when he got there, it turned out to be a personal heaven. With his background in maintenance and his combat record he was made assistant maintenance officer of the Flight Test division. It was not a desk job, there were two hangars full of the latest American and captured German and Japanese fighters. His job was to run functional flight tests on them. It was fun, it was the lifestyle he loved – plenty of flying, plenty of action, plenty of dogfighting. The US Air Force had its own range of jet fighters too, including the P-80, and he tested these alongside the 262s and 163s. He put on flying displays at Wright Field; if anybody needed an aircraft flown for show, there was Yeager, grinning and eager to do it, rolls off the deck, looping at low level. If an aircraft needed to be collected he got the job, because if something went wrong he could usually fix it.

Col. Al Boyd was the chief of Flight Test at Wright Field and he saw the potential in Yeager as a test pilot. He asked him if he would like to go to Test Pilot School and Yeager jumped at the chance. Most of his classmates had degrees and he did have problems on the academic side but that competitive spirit was there to compensate and he qualified as a test pilot in 1946.

The expression 'test pilot' can be misleading. At one end of the scale, there is the production test pilot who flies new aircraft straight off the company's production line. Then there is experimental test pilot who tests and helps develop systems and components. Finally, there is research test pilot who is the ultimate, reaching out into areas where aerodynamic knowledge is scanty or non-existent – the unknown.

In 1947, the Air Corps became the United States Air Force. It did not do research flying, which was left to the company test pilots. Air Force test pilots accepted aircraft from the manufacturers and tested components and Chuck Yeager started his career as an Air Force experimental test pilot, testing gunnery systems for the new jet fighters. But there was one research project which the Air Force was anxious to see pursued as quickly as possible, the X-1 project, which had been started by the Bell Aircraft Company in 1943. The company had been given a government contract to build an aircraft to investigate flight at speeds higher than could be reached in conventional propeller-driven or jet aircraft and, particularly, to research into the question of flying faster than sound. They had built it and the company test pilots had flown it up to around .8 Mach (80 per cent of the speed of sound). But after that, progress had petered out and there was talk of very substantial sums of money changing hands if there was to be any further progress. The Air Force decided to take over the project themselves and Colonel Boyd was given the task of running the practical tests.

There was international competition to be the first to 'break the sound barrier' and the US was in that race. In Britain, the De Havilland company had built a research aircraft for the purpose, the D.H.108. It was jet-powered and took off from the ground in a conventional manner, unlike the X-1 which was rocket-powered and had to be dropped from another aircraft. On 27 September 1946, a D.H.108 carrying out a high-speed flight over the Thames Estuary broke up in flight. The pilot, Geoffrey De Havilland, was killed. A number of pilots had been killed flying at high speeds in dives, trying to find out what happened. Those who survived brought back tales of violent buffeting as they reached the limiting speeds of their aircraft. There were theories about what happened to an aircraft around the speed of sound but there was no hard evidence about the precise nature of the immense loads which were placed on the airframe as it did.

As an aircraft flies through the air, it sends sound waves ahead which warn of its approach, giving the air a chance to divide. The faster an aircraft flies, the shorter the time available for the air ahead to divide and make way for it. Near the speed of sound, it gives no warning of its approach and the sound waves pile up, as snow piles up against a snowplough, creating a barrier. Pushing against the build-up of shock waves was what caused the violent buffeting. The question which could not be answered without pilots putting it to the practical test was: could an aircraft fly through the build-up of sound waves, and, having left them behind, fly on smoothly? That was what the X-1 was built to find out. All it needed was the right pilot.

Colonel Boyd agreed to take on the project. He needed a pilot with a rare combination of qualities: an almost reckless spirit of adventure combined with the discipline and common sense not to take unnecessary risks. He also needed one with a wide enough understanding of engineering to comprehend the problems. Boyd was a wise man, he knew his men and he selected Yeager. He was anxious to have the job done safely, but he was anxious to see it done.

Yeager accepted the job eagerly: it was flying, it looked like fun, it was competitive, both personally and for the Air Force, and it was going into the unknown. And he was getting paid for it; not the huge sums paid to civilian test pilots, just a regular captain's pay of around $200 a month. But it was the lifestyle he loved: he would be with a small, closely-knit team, working very largely on their own initiative with a simple goal of getting the job done. The test site was in California.

The Mojave Desert in Southern California is an empty place, a barren wilderness baked by a merciless sun. High up in this wasteland there is a huge, flat, shimmering expanse, a dry lake-bed called Muroc where the US Army pitched a few tents in 1933 and established a bombing-range. But Muroc was really a great big natural airfield; it was far away from centres of population, under cloudless skies, and the Army quickly saw its potential as a place for experimental flying. By 1947, Muroc Field was a busy and a noisy place: all day long, fighters and bombers came and went, taxiing, taking off and landing, experimental aircraft roared their engines under test; man-made thunder reverberated around the desert.

A pioneering spirit evolved in the X-1 team; they were tackling one of the biggest unknowns in aerodynamics since the Wright Brothers. Was the sound barrier like an invisible brick wall in the sky? Would it ultimately pulverise the X-1 and its pilot or could they find a window in it which would open up a new era in aviation?

There was really only one way to find out, a pilot had to try it. The technique of the research test pilot is to nibble away at a problem, never to bite off more than he can comfortably chew, especially with an aircraft such as the X-1. Rocket-power was new and lethal if not handled very carefully both on the ground and in the air. First, the whole team went back into the classroom to learn about the X-1, its systems, its structure, its known capabilities and its theoretical potential. Flying began with a 'dry' drop, no power at all, just a great big glider flight to give the team a chance to try out the whole system and for Yeager to get the feel of the controls. When they started powered flying, the plan was to increase speed a little at a time.

The first powered flight was made on 29 August 1947. Yeager was briefed very carefully: he was to stay below .8 Mach, he was to test the rocket motor one chamber at a time and get the feel of the aircraft under power. There would be a group of senior officers on the ground to observe the flight and watch him land, and he was briefed to make a fly-past without power before landing.

Everything went according to plan until he had tested the rocket chambers. He tried them one at a time as briefed. They worked fine. Then a little of the Chuck Yeager eagerness and impatience took over. The X-1 was a real aeroplane now, it had power and he just had to fly it a little. Fully laden with fuel, he put it into a slow roll and for a few glorious moments he was weightless, floating in his seat, the centre of his own little surreal world. Then the engine cut and he went into a dive with the group of senior officers waiting far below on the airfield for a glide-past and landing. He continued to dive, then levelled off at 5000 feet over the airfield, silent as a bird. Then his fingers reached for the igniter switches and he fired the first chamber, putting the X-1 into a shallow climb; just to give the observers a little treat. Then he closed the second switch, then the third, then the fourth. As the power roared on and acceleration increased he had to keep the nose coming up and up, into an ever-steeper climb, to avoid exceeding the authorised Mach number of .8. Soon he was flying straight up in a 90-degree climb and still accelerating. He pulled over the top as if beginning a huge loop, then rolled out at 30,000 feet and cut the motor with the Machmeter showing .85 Mach. Chuck Yeager was on top of the world. This was fun.

After that, he increased speed a little on each flight, going a little further into the buffet. Then, on the seventh flight, when he had worked up to .94 Mach he hit a snag: when he tried the controls he found that he had virtually no elevator effectiveness; when he pulled back on the control column there was no change in the attitude of the aircraft. What predictions there were about the likely behaviour of the X-1 as it approached the speed of sound suggested that it would be liable to a lot of pitching, the nose moving up and down relative to straight and level flight, and without effective elevators Yeager would have no means to control it. The shock wave which the X-1 was producing at that speed had moved back along the tailplane to the elevators and it was flattening out, gripping them like a vice. The X-1 had been built with a moveable tailplane which had not been used up to then. He decided to try moving it in flight, using the whole tailplane as an elevator.

He took it up and accelerated to .94 Mach. There was really no way he could be certain what would happen: he might regain some control over the pitching, or he might spin out of control. It worked, and from then on he used the whole tailplane as an elevator for speeds above .94 Mach.

Life was not all high-speed flight, earnest scientific deliberation and engineering experiment; there was a lighter side to life at Muroc in the form of a special pub which the pilots frequented. It was called Pancho's Fly Inn, owned and run by a formidable lady, Pancho Barnes, who had been a record-breaking pilot and barnstormer. She had promised a free steak dinner to the pilot who broke the sound barrier and lived to tell her the tale. Chuck and Glennis went over to Pancho's to ride horses and, going flat out on his horse as he did in his aeroplane, one Monday night, Yeager collided with a gate, fell off and damaged his ribs.

When he got to the airfield the following morning, 14 October 1947, he knew that if he went to the doctor on the base he would be pronounced unfit to fly. He was determined that nobody else would replace him, so he went to a civilian doctor some way away and had his ribs taped up. He told his friend, the engineer Jack Ridley, of the problems and Ridley sawed the end off a broomstick so that he could use it to close the door. He hid the broomstick, and his pain, and climbed aboard the B-29 bomber, which carried the X-1 aloft.

About 10.15 the air above Muroc stilled, aircraft cleared the area, engines on the ground were cut, the bustle subsided; there was an air of expectancy; a test flight was about to take place. Just visible overhead, the lone B-29 Superfortress climbed steadily into a quartz-blue sky. Close by were two even smaller specks – two jet fighters acting as chase aircraft.

Inside the perspex bubble-nose of the bomber the air was cold, but the sun warmed the crew as they went through the familiar routine with their usual, unhurried professionalism. Behind the flight crew, Chuck Yeager sat in his usual place on a little bench. Slung in the B-29's belly was the sleek X-1 with *Glamorous Glennis* painted on the nose.

As the B-29 clambered past 10,000 feet, Yeager got up and went back into the bomb bay. Inside, it was noisy and even colder: the doors had been removed and there was a narrow catwalk round the X-1 which hung, shackled like a bomb, in the slipstream. Between the catwalk and the X-1 there was a gap, big enough for a man to get through, and the desert was visible far below. The X-1 was painted bright orange, but around its waist there was a white band of frozen condensation where the liquid oxygen tank had cooled the skin of the aircraft from the inside.

To get into the X-1 Yeager braced himself against the slipstream then climbed down a short ladder and crawled through a door in the side of the aircraft into the tiny cockpit. It was dark inside: he plugged in his intercom and oxygen tube and strapped in. The engineer, Jack Ridley, then passed down the door and Yeager locked it from the inside, using the broomstick to lever the lock into position. His eyes grew accustomed to the dark; he checked the instruments.

'Checklist complete,' he reported to the B-29 pilot, Cardenas.

'Roger,' replied Yeager.

The two chase aircraft positioned themselves – one behind the B-29 and one in front.

Yeager pressurised the fuel tanks and tested the fuel jettison system.

'Two minutes to drop,' said Cardenas.

He sat and waited. Ridley had removed the last umbilical hoses and the X-1 now relied on its own power supply: the systems were powered up, the needles of the instruments were alive. He felt the B-29 go into a shallow dive to give the X-1 more speed as it dropped away from the mother aircraft.

Cardenas counted down the final seconds: '10-9-8-7-6-5-4-3-2-1 Drop!'

The shackles let got with a dull snap and the X-1 dropped like a bomb, throwing Yeager briefly up in his seat; in the same moment the dark interior was suddenly filled with brilliant sunlight.

In the silent cockpit Yeager could hear the movie cameras whirring away, recording everything he did. He closed a switch which started the first motor, firing the liquid oxygen and a mixture of water and alcohol; then he switched on the second. The X-1 leapt forward, it was a thoroughbred now, a real aeroplane, he was forced back into his seat by the acceleration even though he was climbing; in a matter of seconds his speed had doubled. He fired the next two rocket chambers and it reached full power. Once again he was pushed back into his seat. It was as if unseen forces were trying to tear the X-1 apart, the aircraft was shuddering violently, like driving a car flat out over a rough road. Yeager stayed quite calm; he concentrated on the controls. He switched off two of the motors in the climb before levelling off at 42,000 feet. The Machmeter showed .92 Mach – 92 per cent of the speed of sound. He switched on the third rocket chamber in level flight and accelerated rapidly again. The Machmeter moved up to .93 Mach; he anticipated the loss of elevator effectiveness and adjusted the tailplane. Yeager did not know what to expect; he was going into the unknown; the Machmeter showed .96 Mach; he was still in control and he actually found that the elevators were regaining their effectiveness. That was new. Suddenly, the Machmeter needle fluctuated then shot off the end of the scale, equivalent to 1.05 Mach, around 700 miles an hour. It was a serene rather than a startling moment; the buffeting had stopped and Chuck Yeager was flying faster than sound – the first man ever to do so.

He had agreed a code with the rest of the team, to let them know without announcing it to the world: 'Make a note, there's something wrong with the Machmeter, it's gone screwy.'

That meant he had done it. Typically, he was a little disappointed that the breakthrough had not been more dramatic. The fuel ran out and he was still going up. He was pleased that the job had been done and allowed himself a little celebration: the X-1 was a beautiful aeroplane and this was his moment; up in the thin air against the indigo sky he flew for fun, rolling and looping the X-1 before gliding in to land.

Back on the ground they called Colonel Boyd and gave him the news. Within hours a call came back putting a complete ban on any kind of comment outside those who already knew. It was to be a total secret. But that night, secret or not, Yeager went to Pancho's for his steak dinner.

The aviation fraternity knew that a breakthrough of some kind had been made at Muroc but they only had rumours to go on. There was speculative coverage in the aviation press, but the Air Force doggedly refused to acknowledge that one of its pilots had flown one of its aircraft faster than sound. The reason they were so secret was, in essence, the same reason that Orville and Wilbur Wright had kept their flights quiet: they did not want the competition to get to know either precisely what they had done or, more importantly, how they had done it. In this case, the competition was Communist Russia. America had a whole series of jet fighters in production and on the drawing-board and they wanted time to incorporate what they had learned on the X-1 into the designs. One aircraft in particular benefited from the concept of the moveable tailplane. The F-86 Sabre which became one of the mainstays of the US Air Force fighter fleet had a moveable tailplane, and when it came up against the MiG-15 in the Korean War, though it was inferior in some respects, in high-speed performance it had the edge.

The Air Force went public in June 1948 and admitted to the world that it had 'broken the sound barrier' and Yeager was publicly honoured and rewarded with medals and trophies. But his achievement was nine months old, it had been made in secret, and even when they announced it, the full details were not given. On top of that, by then he was not the only pilot who had flown faster than sound. Consequently he did not become an instant popular hero like Lindbergh; he remained what he had always been, an Air Force insider, doing his job, drawing his pay, flying all he could and enjoying the lifestyle.

The late 1940s and early 1950s were years of great progress in high-speed flying and a great deal of fundamental aerodynamic research, exploring the frontier between pure theory and practice, was done at Muroc Field, or Edwards Air Force Base as it was renamed in 1949 after a test pilot, Glen Edwards, who was killed on a test flight. Yeager stayed at Edwards for seven years after his first supersonic flight. He loved it there: it was a competitive atmosphere, he was right at the top of the profession of research-flying and his reputation grew and grew within the service. He made thirty more flights in the X-1, twelve of them supersonic, and then there followed a whole range of other experimental aircraft.

But as the demands of aerodynamic research increased, so Edwards itself grew and grew, until there was little left of the pioneering spirit of the small team which had started research-flying in the Air Force. There was companionship between research pilots, but it was not the tightly-knit group which Yeager had started out with; it was still competitive, possibly even more so as other pilots came along. On 20 November 1953, a civilian test pilot, Scott Crossfield, set a new record when he flew the Douglas D-558-2 to twice the speed of sound. Three weeks later, on 12 December, Yeager went out to get the record back for the Air Force in a derivative of the X-1, the X-1A.

The X-1A was designed to fly at Mach 2, twice the speed of sound. Like its predecessor, the X-1, it had to be borne aloft by another aircraft and dropped. After the drop, Yeager switched on all four rocket chambers and climbed swiftly to over 70,000 feet. He accelerated to 2.4 Mach, well over the design speed for the aircraft. At that speed, the skin heated up from the friction with the air, even though the air at that height was extremely thin. When the fuel ran out, the X-1A slowed down to around Mach 1 quite safely, then, suddenly, he lost control and the aircraft started tumbling down from over 70,000 feet. Yeager was thrown around inside the cockpit, against the hot skin of the aircraft and against the canopy; eventually he lost consciousness. He came to at 25,000 feet, battered and bruised and falling fast. He gasped into the radio to let the chase aircraft know where he was and then managed to glide back to base, without power, to land. He admitted that if he had had an ejector seat, he would have used it. He had been into the unknown again – at that height, the air had been just too thin for the X-1A to remain under control.

In 1954, Yeager went back to a fighter squadron. It was a part of the Air Force he loved, but it was rather different from 1944. He was stationed in Germany to start with, the old enemy; the squadron flew the F-86 Sabre jet fighters and he was a lieutenant colonel, in command. Then he came back to California to command a squadron of F-100 Super Sabres, the first front-line jet fighter to be capable of supersonic speeds in level flight.

In 1960, he was sent back to Edwards. There was a new rocket-powered aircraft in the X-series, the X-15, which was classified as hypersonic, capable of speeds in excess of six times the speed of sound, over 4000 miles an hour, and reaching altitudes of fifty miles, the frontier between the atmosphere and space. The manned space programme was under way too and even in its infancy, in the early 1960s, the emphasis was shifting to rockets which propelled a capsule into orbit rather than a rocket aircraft like the X series. Yeager was a pilot, he liked to control the aircraft he was flying and did not want to become an astronaut.

There were still some records to be broken inside the atmosphere. In 1961, the Russians held the altitude record for an aircraft which took off under its own power – 113,000 feet. The X-2 and the X-15 had flown higher but they had been air-launched. There was a research aircraft at Edwards which could possibly fly higher, all it needed was somebody to try it. It was the NF-104, a converted fighter with an ordinary jet engine with afterburner and a rocket engine as well. It had an additional control system, too, since the air was so thin at those altitudes that conventional controls were ineffective. It had little thruster nozzles which could be moved to different angles to change direction in the thin air. Yeager had already flown it to 108,000 feet and going that little bit further was too much of a temptation.

He took off and climbed at 2.2 Mach to over 60,000 feet on the jet engine with afterburner. Then he switched to the rocket motor and felt a great surge of new power pushing into his back as he climbed on to over 100,000 feet, where he cut the motors. Still climbing in a great arc, he passed 104,000 feet, operating the thrusters to bring the nose down. They had no effect; the nose stayed up. He had already been to 108,000 where the air was even thinner, but at 104,000, there was just enough air to give some resistance. The nose stayed up in the air as the aircraft began to slide backwards towards the ground, then suddenly went into a flat spin. Round and round he went, black sky, bright earth flashing past. He struggled with the controls, trying every trick in his repertoire, but to no effect. He could not restart the jet engine unless he could get the nose down and he could not get out of the spin without power. He deployed the brake parachute which snatched the aircraft out of the spin and pointed the nose down, then jettisoned the 'chute. The aircraft promptly went back into the nose-up attitude again; the control surfaces were frozen into a nose-up position. Finally, he pulled the ring and operated the ejector seat and was punched out just 7000 feet above the ground. Spent rocket fuel from the ejector seat dribbled into his helmet and all over his parachute lines, burning his face and hands. He was severely injured but landed safely and was picked up by a rescue helicopter.

Not long afterwards, the rocket aircraft programme was brought to an end as the emphasis was placed more and more on the Gemini and Apollo space programmes. Before it was quite over, the X-15 flew at 6.72 Mach and climbed to over 354,000 feet, well beyond what was officially regarded as the atmosphere. But by now the new frontier in aviation was beyond that. The new frontier was in orbit. Even if he had wanted to, Chuck Yeager could not have been one of the first seven astronauts because he did not have a college degree which was a requirement. He was made commander of the Aerospace Research Pilots' School at Edwards, responsible for training the cream of the military test pilots. Thirty-eight of his graduates finished up in the space programme.

Then in the late 1960s, America was at war again, this time in Vietnam. Chuck Yeager went back to combat-flying and he flew on over a hundred tactical bombing missions in South-East Asia.

For four decades Chuck Yeager has been a legend growing in the small world of research test-flying and as a fighter pilot, but it was only very recently that he became anything of a popular hero. When Tom Wolfe wrote *The Right Stuff*, the definitive account of the first astronauts who were drawn from the ranks of military test pilots, he used Chuck Yeager as the benchmark against which all test pilots had to be measured for the personal qualities needed for the job. He is the ultimate example of that rare combination of qualities which are required for the most demanding flying job. He has them in plenty and dispenses them with ease: coolness and calmness far beyond simple personal courage, especially under

the pressure of falling out of the sky in an aerodynamically interesting experiment. He is over sixty years old and still has that
can-do philosophy of life. He is still flying and testing high-
performance jet fighters such as the F-20. He goes hunting,
shooting and fishing in the mountains, but they are the mountains
of northern California now, not too far away from Edwards where
he remains a frequent visitor. He still has his lifestyle just the way
he wants it.

9 John Young

Cape Canaveral is a watery place, a spit of land between the hard, Atlantic shoreline and the swampy banks of the Banana and Indian Rivers; along their banks and in the creeks, a rich variety of wildlife thrives in the natural and man-made pools. Man is not a newcomer: the early Spanish settlers once lived on the shore and there were Indian communities in the area for many centuries before that. But in the last four decades man has changed the face of the Cape completely, building great islands of concrete linked by roads and bridges; tall girder structures stick up confidently across the landscape of Cape Canaveral, the home of America's Spaceport, the Kennedy Space Center.

When President Kennedy took office in 1961, it was just plain Cape Canaveral, a rather shabby place where the US armed forces had been testing rockets since the end of the Second World War. In 1961, America was locked into the 'Cold War', an arms race with Russia, a period characterised by spine-chilling rhetoric and rivalry in every field: political, economic and technical. Neither superpower was prepared to let the other dominate in any field and that included what Kennedy called 'the new frontier' – space. 1961 was the year that the 'space race' became a reality.

The Russians were first away: on 12 April 1961, Yuri Gagarin orbited the Earth once, remaining in space for 1 hour 48 minutes.

Three weeks later, Alan Shepard was launched on America's first flight into space in *Freedom 7*. It was a much shorter flight, just 15 minutes, and it was simply up from Cape Canaveral and down into the Atlantic Ocean.

It was nearly a year before America matched the Russian achievement when John Glenn, the all-American US Marine fighter pilot, orbited the Earth, the first American to do so. There were just seven astronauts in America at that time and their flights in the Mercury programme were the breakthrough; they gave America a foothold in space and demonstrated that America could match the Russian technology and effort.

Aviation, or aerospace as it has become known, has always been highly political, with all its implications for national security and ultimate potential for commercialisation. Exploring new frontiers has become too expensive for most companies, let alone individuals, and space flight in the 1960s was beyond the pocket of anybody without the backing of a rich and advanced economy. In a mood of fear of Russian intentions in space, coupled with a sense of national pride in its technical ability and a touch of national and political exuberance, President Kennedy committed the United States to a goal which seemed to many people to come straight out of science fiction – to land a man on the Moon before the end of the decade. It was a clearly identifiable goal and a gesture of complete faith in America's ability to meet the huge technical challenge. But to do it, they would also need some more astronauts.

In September 1962, a second batch of nine astronauts was chosen, the Gemini nine. Among them were names which would go on to make space history: Neil Armstrong, Frank Borman, Charles Conrad, James Lovell, Ed White, James McDivitt, Tom Stafford and, last alphabetically, and quietest of them all in the ballyhoo which surrounded their sudden projection into the public and political arena – John Young.

He was thirty-two years old with impeccable qualifications to be an astronaut: he was a navy test pilot and he came from test-flying the double-sonic Phantom, the most advanced fighter of its time; he had graduated from flying jet fighters from aircraft carriers, one of the most tricky flying jobs. He had a fine academic record too: a degree in aeronautical engineering from Georgia Tech and a long history of classroom and sporting achievement before that at his high school in Orlando, Florida, which he left as 'Most Outstanding Scholar' in 1948 with a reputation for quietness of manner and application to work.

The Gemini programme was a bridge between the one-man flights of the Mercury programme and the three-man Apollo Moon-landing programme. It was a highly technical programme whose purpose was to learn about flying and working in space. Unlike the Russians who concentrated more on automated systems, the American astronauts decided early on that human input would be important and the Gemini programme relied heavily on astronauts learning to think and act in space, using the technology but retaining the pilot's ability to take over at any time. It was an intensive programme; in less than two years there were ten flights and in that time America gradually overhauled the

Russians in both technology and human expertise, striving to fulfil President Kennedy's national objective.

John Young was the pilot on the first manned mission in the programme, *Gemini 3*, in March 1965; the commander was 'Gus' Grissom. The capsule on top of the Titan rocket which carried the two pilots was about the size of a very small car with no rear seats, and the interior was crammed with instruments. His first flight was a short one: three orbits of the Earth lasting just 4 hours, 53 minutes. But it was a significant one: there was a thruster system on board which enabled the pilots to change the orbit of the capsule as they wished, flying the spacecraft rather than being simply baggage in the hold of a vehicle sent on an automatically predetermined trip. Young's first flight gave him a taste for space: he liked the weightlessness, he liked the spaceman's view of the world, he liked working with systems; there was a computer on board which enabled the pilots to work out how much thrust to apply and when. Young liked making the technology work, using his own expertise to get it to perform as well as possible, and *Gemini 3* splashed down right on time and right on target.

When they came back from the first Gemini flight, Grissom and Young became instant national heroes. Astronauts were part of the ammunition in the public relations battle of the Cold War and in a country which adores its heroes, they were superheroes. Grissom had experienced the full blast of public adulation before, on the Mercury programme, but nothing in Young's life had prepared him for it. In the highly-charged international atmosphere, achievement in space flight was high-value political currency and only days before, the Russian cosmonaut, Alexei Leonov, had made the first ever spacewalk; Grissom and Young had snatched back the limelight. Part of Young's job now was to ride with politicians: he and Grissom met President Johnson, they rode in a ticker tape parade through Manhattan in the limousine with Vice-President Humphrey and appeared on public platforms to say a few words which always brought a cheer. The inwardly tough but outwardly reserved and thoughtful John Young was out of his depth; the supercool pilot was awkward in front of the crowds.

Outwardly he may have been modest, even shy, but he did not join the élite band of aviators who became astronauts by being a shrinking violet; he got there through his career as a test pilot, flying to the limits and beyond. Within the security of the astronaut community he was confident and ambitious and in the highly competitive world of space flight, where getting on a mission was every pilot's goal, he saw that success would come from hard work and skill and demonstrating his mastery of the technology to those who did the selecting. Astronauts were highly trained pilots before they started space training, when they were put through the most rigorous new schedule; if anything, they were overtrained for the job, but they were going into the unknown and it was better to be safe than sorry. John Young took part in experiments which were designed to solve some of the basic engineering problems of flying and working in space: he worked with space tools while suspended on a cable, he worked underwater in a spacesuit to simulate weightlessness, and when a test was needed to determine what level of oscillation a pilot could stand in a Gemini capsule before he lost the ability to read the instruments, he was put in a centrifuge and spun round to induce the high G forces associated with space flight, then shaken violently at eleven cycles per second, at which point the instrument panel became unreadable.

One technique which was vital to both sides in the space race was the ability for two spacecraft to rendezvous in space and dock with each other. Such a technique would be useful in Earth orbit so that manned spacecraft could link up with space laboratories but it was crucial for the Moon-landing programme.

Gemini 6 and *7*, both manned, managed to rendezvous with each other. *Gemini 8* managed to rendezvous and dock with an unmanned Agena rocket which had been launched for the purpose but once the docking was complete, the linked spacecraft began tumbling and spinning out of control and the astronauts, Neil Armstrong and David Scott, narrowly averted a tragedy by firing their retrorockets to disengage. *Gemini 9* failed to rendezvous with its Agena, so the task of making another attempt fell to John Young as commander of *Gemini 10* and his co-pilot Michael Collins.

Young and Collins were launched from Cape Canaveral in July 1966. They started out in a relatively low orbit, scanning the dark horizon for the Agena through their little windows and with radar. They could see for thousands of miles in the perfect clearness of space; the Earth was bright and the 'sky' of deep space was very dark. They found the Agena and when Young had eye-contact, he began the tricky manoeuvre of docking: he operated the little thrusters, puffing the capsule gently into the right position and attitude relative to the Agena, coasting ever so gently towards it, then finally nosing into it and locking the two craft together. There was no tumble; he had done it. Next, he used the Agena's motor to propel the combined craft into a much higher orbit, 761 kilometres above the Earth. In their new orbit, Young docked with a second Agena, the one left by *Gemini 8*, then Collins 'spacewalked' over to it and retrieved a package which had been collecting dust particles.

The flight lasted three days, three days sitting in a very cramped capsule carrying out delicate operations involving both physical skill and mental dexterity. It was no place for a pilot with an impatient nature or one irritated by close confinement. The flight was a complete success; not only did it demonstrate that the policy of having trained men who could fly their spacecraft was paying off; it was the clearest demonstration yet that in both technical and human terms, the Americans were overtaking the Russians. It was 1969 before the Russians managed to dock two spacecraft in space.

On the technical side the Americans were winning, and they were winning on the public relations side too. The motives behind the funding of the space race and its rapid progress were political and international; the means of conducting the race was highly technical; the energy and enthusiasm which made them work and the cost other than in money was very human. In April 1967 the Russians had a tragedy when one of their experienced cosmonauts, Vladimir Komarov, was killed on a space flight, the first operational death in space. Komarov's death was a stern reminder of the dangers involved in reaching for new horizons.

While the Gemini programme was teaching astronauts about flying and working in space, the next lap of the race was being planned. The Apollo programme was intended to fulfil President Kennedy's goal of landing a man on the Moon before the end of the decade. The Apollo spacecraft was a huge tower of combustible materials, 350 feet high, consisting of four major parts: at the top was the command module which was broadly similar in appearance to the Gemini capsules though much larger and designed to carry three men, the commander, the lunar module pilot and the command module pilot; beneath was the service module containing the rocket motors which would bring the astronauts back from the Moon; behind came the lunar module containing the fragile two-stage system which would take two of the astronauts down to the Moon and back up again, and behind that were the three stages of the giant Saturn rocket which would carry it all into Earth orbit and then fire it towards the Moon.

Apollo 10 was launched in May 1969, the second manned flight to the Moon and the last before *Apollo 11* which finally landed men on the surface. The commander was Tom Stafford, the lunar module pilot was Eugene Cernan and the command module pilot was John Young. Once they were safely in transit towards the Moon, it was Young's job to separate the command and service module from the lunar module, turn round, dock with it again, then extract the fragile lunar landing-craft from its housing. Once that process was complete, the crew could settle down to a routine for the two-day flight to the Moon.

They had the first colour television camera to go on a lunar flight and as they left the Earth, they sent back the most beautiful pictures of the watery, cloudy planet, turning and shrinking as they sped away. They put on an impromptu variety show, the evocative shots of the Earth were intercut with scenes of the weightless astronauts demonstrating the fun side of being in space. Young turned somersaults and worked his way upside down in the cramped capsule; Cernan, who was right way up in the picture, pushed him gently on his head, up to the top of the picture; all three astronauts played weightless frisbee with pieces of equipment, making them collide and spin off in all directions. They played 'Fly Me to the Moon', sung by Frank Sinatra, over a crackling radio link with Earth and Young held up pictures from the Peanuts cartoon of the flight mascots, which showed Charlie Brown and Snoopy in his traditional World War I flying-kit in search of the Red Baron. The Americans were ahead in the technical space race, but in public relations they were now in a class of their own.

The television spectacular continued in lunar orbit: while Cernan and Stafford went down to within nine kilometres of the Sea of Tranquillity to examine the *Apollo 11* landing-site, John Young sent back stunning colour pictures of the surface, a bright milky-marbly landscape, pitted with craters and scarred by sharp mountain ridges, rolling by under a black sky. Man's greatest feat of exploration was beamed direct into the world's sitting-rooms; while the crew worked on in precarious surroundings a quarter of a million miles from home, millions watched the vulnerable-looking lunar landing-craft ease up from its look at the surface of the Moon and dock with the command module.

The rest, as they say, is history. *Apollo 10* returned safely and two months later, *Apollo 11* landed Neil Armstrong and 'Buzz' Aldrin on the Moon, fulfilling President Kennedy's goal with just five months to spare.

The following year, the risks of operating at the frontiers of aeronautical knowledge were demonstrated when a fuel tank exploded on *Apollo 13* while heading for the Moon and the crew had to go all the way into lunar orbit, getting colder and colder to conserve fuel, then use the lunar landing-module to tow them back to Earth. It was the nearest America had come to a space disaster and had it not been for the personal ingenuity of the crew and the technicians on the ground, it would have been fatal.

John Young got his chance to walk on the Moon in 1972 as commander of *Apollo 16*, the last but one of the Moon landings. It was a mission beset by technical problems from the start: when they removed the lunar landing-module from its stowage, paint flaked off; the navigation system in the command module failed; a steerable aerial jammed, and when they were in lunar orbit and Young and the lunar module pilot Duke had separated from the command module, things got worse.

They separated in an elliptical orbit but before the lunar module set out for the surface of the Moon, the command module pilot, Ken Mattingly, had to boost himself into a circular orbit. When he tested the back-up system for firing the rocket motor, there was an indication of an oscillation in the main engine, the one which would have to fly them all back to Earth. With only minutes to go, Mission Control told them to hold off while they tried to sort out the problem. For six hours, the two craft remained separated while orbiting the Moon together as Mission Control and Mattingly worked on the problem which they eventually solved.

The lunar landing-craft was a frail machine; it looked like a rather battered aluminium box. It was a tiny capsule which landed on a cushion of rocket power aimed at the ground; it was fragile because it was designed to operate solely in the low gravity on the Moon. Their landing-site was in the Descartes Crater and as it neared the surface, the pilots judged their landing by watching the dust blow away as it settled on to the surface.

John Young had the time of his life on the Moon; he and Duke spent over twenty hours exploring and carrying out experiments. They set up television cameras to record their activities for the audience back home, then they put up the Stars and Stripes and saluted; Mission Control guided Young to a particular rock in the foreground of the picture which had caught the eye of the geologists and he picked it up. Exploring in the Moon buggy was great fun and Young gave the audience a treat when he drove the electric car at full tilt, churning up the sandy surface. In all, they collected 97 kilogrammes of Moon rock. The cameras were left on to capture the launch of the ascent stage of the lunar module.

The Americans were clearly masters of space flight at that time, but after one more Apollo mission the programme was closed down. In the same period, Russia had two spectacular failures and four of its cosmonauts were killed in two separate accidents. The American programme had been successful but there was little profit or obvious direct benefit from continuing to fly to the Moon and it was enormously expensive. They had demonstrated that man could live and work in space but the government and the people of America were looking for something new and more substantial in return for their investment than stunning television pictures and a few sacks full of Moon rock. In the 1970s, the space programme wound down and many of the pioneering astronauts headed for business, politics or retirement.

But not John Young. There was a new programme in the making; the Shuttle was still on the drawing-board. America was planning a reusable spacecraft; one which took off like a rocket but which landed like an aeroplane; one which could begin regular flights into space for commercial and military purposes. It was a huge engineering project and was beset with problems; but it was the only way for a keen astronaut to get back into space. In January 1973 John Young was assigned to the Shuttle project. His job was to feed into the design not only his engineering expertise and experience, but also to give the astronaut's point of view of how best to arrange things; it was fertile ground for his type of mind.

Two years later he eased himself in front of the whole team to become chief of the Astronaut Office, a perfect position from which to stake his claim for the job of test-flying the Shuttle and getting back into space.

In 1980, he reached his fiftieth birthday but he was still superbly fit; he spent many of his few leisure hours running and water-skiing. He needed the stamina of fitness because he had to keep up his training and compete with younger men too; he went underwater in a spacesuit to test, among other things, a manual system for closing the payload bay doors if they jammed open in space; over and over again, he practised getting out of his space-suit in the back of a converted Boeing 707 airliner as it flew in a parabolic curve to give astronauts around forty seconds of weight-lessness to train in. He flew over a thousand hours in the Shuttle flight simulator and flew it on piggyback rides atop a converted jumbo jet.

John Young, the quiet man, is a sticker; he has a knack of getting his own way in the astronaut business; he had been an astronaut for eighteen years and though there were others on the active list who may have thought that they should have got the first flight, on

12 April 1981 it was John Young who was sitting on the launch pad waiting for lift-off.

Early that morning the area around the Cape was teeming with people. Long before the first orange light of a Florida dawn had stirred the birds and insects, the roads and car parks were full and the smell of hamburgers mixed with the dewy-damp of early morning. Every vantage point for miles around was taken up with people; thousands of cameras pointed towards the Cape. It was the day for another Space Spectacular, the first flight of the world's first reusable spaceship, the Space Shuttle, a multi-billion-dollar machine which went up like a rocket but landed like an aeroplane. For a society addicted to novelty and one which believes profoundly in progress through technology, the lure of the Shuttle and the prospect that it would usher in a new era in space exploration and, possibly more importantly, space exploi-tation, was too strong to resist. Over a million Americans made the pilgrimage to Cape Canaveral to see the launch with their own eyes.

Live television relayed the scene at Launch Complex 39A to millions more in America and around the world. From privileged positions inside the perimeter fence, the eyes of the world looked on: reporters and photographers sat and waited in special galler-ies; cameramen tested their equipment for the umpteenth time as the sun came up and commentators struggled to evoke the atmos-phere of the occasion. The gleaming white Shuttle standing in majestic splendour before the world seemed for a moment to be America's equivalent of the approaching British Royal Wedding, an opportunity to show the world a potent symbol of national pride.

Technicians swarmed all over the launch pad, but as their final checks were made, they gradually thinned out and in the full light of day the Shuttle stood alone, a stirring testimony to America's technical heritage. Tension mounted as the launch time approached; the television cameras switched periodically from long-lens shots of the Shuttle to scenes inside the control rooms where hundreds more NASA technicians sat hunched over their visual display units. Television viewers heard the disembodied voices chattering across the airwaves as they monitored the count-down and checked the seemingly endless technical details.

From those same control rooms, the lines of communication hummed round the world, voices and electronic messages carried to tracking stations on other continents, to ships at sea, to weather aircraft, to Mission Control in Houston, Texas, to the Department of Defense, the State Department and through them to foreign governments, to the Coast Guard, to Search and Rescue teams and to the two pilots in the Shuttle itself.

There were no unmanned test flights, the first ever flight of the Shuttle was manned. The flight deck looked rather like an ultra-modern airliner: two pilots, seated side by side, separated by a console packed with instruments. There the similarity ended: the pilots were dressed in spacesuits and helmets and they were lying on their backs in ejector seats. In the right-hand seat lay Bob Crippen on his first space flight; in the left-hand seat lay John Young, America's chief astronaut, about to make his fifth space flight.

John Young was fifty years old and he wore glasses; his quiet manner did not change as the time for the launch drew nearer, and the technicians monitoring his heartbeat saw it rise from 60 beats a minute to a mere 85; Crippen's rose to 130.

Young sounded calm and professional over the radio. He *was* calm, because that was the way he was, not because he was oblivious to the dangers of making the first flight in a machine as complex as the Shuttle. He understood the problems better than anybody.

He understood the problems because he had lost a close collea-gue when something had gone wrong. In 1967, 'Gus' Grissom, with whom he had made his first space flight in *Gemini 3*, and two other astronauts, Ed White and Roger Chaffee, were killed on the launch pad when an electrical fault ignited the rocket fuel and consumed their Apollo spacecraft in an instant inferno.

He understood the complexity of the Space Shuttle because he had been intimately concerned throughout its development. It was the most complicated aircraft ever built: a huge structure contain-ing a maze of interdependent systems: propulsion, fuel, navi-gation, communications, hydraulic, electronic, pneumatic, environmental, life-support, waste-management, gas-purge, vent, drain and avionic systems. On the outside of the Orbiter there was a huge external fuel tank full of liquid oxygen and hydrogen with attendant high-pressure pumps and igniters; strapped to the side of that were two solid fuel booster rockets.

At 7.00 a.m. the rocket motors roared into life, billowing smoke across the ponds of Cape Canaveral; birds rose into the air in alarm. The Shuttle lifted off, trailing a bright flame across the sky. The atmosphere of the Cape and on television was one of promise and excitement at the dawning of a new space age. As it cleared the tower, thousands of cameras clicked to capture one of the most vivid images of the power of technology. Millions more round the world marvelled as the great white machine rolled gracefully round until the pilots' heads were back pointing towards the Earth and it disappeared from sight.

Twelve minutes later the Shuttle was in space; the solid booster rockets and the external fuel tank, their fuel expended, had dropped away. John Young was back in space after a nine-year break and he was flying the first real spaceship on its first orbital flight. In the years of development there had been many problems and the Shuttle project had been dogged by speculation about its viability. But when it was up, America rejoiced in a technical triumph, the logical next step in the space race, a space bus and truck; the first step towards a new dimension in another American dream, the commercialisation of space. Apart from launching and servicing satellites, it could bring them back; it could take up experiments for processing materials such as pharmaceuticals in zero gravity, and looking further into the future, it could carry components and the labour force to build space stations for permanent habitation and as stepping-stones in the exploration of deeper space.

John Young and Bob Crippen spent two days checking the Shuttle over in space, working the systems, the cargo bay doors and the computers. Then they faced the ultimate test: re-entry and a landing back on Earth like an aeroplane. One of the features of the Shuttle was its coating of silica tiles which soaked up the heat on re-entry. Previous spacecraft had burned up the heat shield which meant that they could not be used again. The tiles were the key to the success of the Shuttle and on the launch, some of them had been torn off.

Young and Crippen went through their drills for re-entry: they fired one set of rockets to slow the Shuttle down from its orbital speed of 17,500 miles per hour, then another set to roll it upright in relation to the Earth. Over the western Pacific Ocean they began to re-enter the atmosphere. Far below they could see the ocean; clouds which looked high from the surface of the Earth appeared as white flecks on a bright sea stretching as far as the gently curved horizon. The tiles worked well, despite the damage. Back in the atmosphere the Shuttle could be controlled like an aeroplane, but it had no power; it was a 99-ton glider with a whole ocean to cross. As it flew over the Pacific, the speed gradually dropped from 18 Mach to 4 Mach over the western coast of America. Over land Young turned the Shuttle and they lost even more speed and a fighter came alongside, photographing the damage to the tiles.

The Shuttle had a glide path six times steeper than an airliner and no power; Young had only one chance of making a landing. Twenty-five minutes after re-entering the atmosphere over the western Pacific, it touched down on the dry lake-bed at Muroc, in the Mojave Desert, Edwards Air Force Base, the site of so many American triumphs in aviation. Over a quarter of a million people drove out into the wilderness to watch, and once again most of the rest of the world was watching on television.

The name John Young was on every commentator's lips; he was the man of the moment, the hero. But a more unlikely hero it is difficult to imagine. In interviews his responses are quiet, thoughtful, and could have come straight out of a NASA public relations handout. If an interviewer strays too far from the matter in hand – the future of the space programme – he is sure to be quietly but firmly evaded.

There is a fleet of four Orbiters now, the Space Shuttle is in regular use and the men who fly it today are routine space pilots. It carries passengers, scientific experts, payload specialists, technicians, America's first female astronaut, a US Senator and even a few foreign nationals. The US Government has given a tentative go-ahead for the building of a space station and the prospect of permanent habitation in space is looming ever nearer. When it does, there will be Shuttle pilots like there are airline pilots today.

When near-Earth space flight is commonplace, there will still be opportunities for pilots like John Young to take the next great leap forward in aerospace, flying into deep space and orbiting the near planets. The centenary of the Wright Brothers' flight will undoubtedly be celebrated at a cocktail party in orbit. Among the guests will be a few of the pilots with that same rare combination of qualities which makes them strive for new horizons in aviation.

Postscript

Progress – as Mr Tom Smallways, the greengrocer in H. G. Wells's novel *The War in the Air*, observed – keeps on; he marvelled at it; it just kept on. That was in 1908, just as aircraft were making their début on the stage of progress, when only the rarest of minds could visualise the effect they would have, not only on the conduct of war, but also on the way we live and on our perception of the world.

From the perspective of the other end of the twentieth century, it is harder to visualise a world without aircraft than it is to imagine what progress aviation will bring in the next century.

Pioneering research in aeronautics goes on to find new applications for aircraft – short and vertical take-off transports, monster, hydrogen-powered airliners, etc. The use of military aircraft – fighters, bombers, transports, helicopters – is central to tactical and strategic philosophy: the job which men like Richthofen did in 1915 – observation from aircraft – is being done today by satellites and just as fighters were developed to shoot down the observers, so 'killer' satellites, or possibly manned spacecraft like the Shuttle, will one day shoot down observation satellites. Civil aircraft continue to shrink the Earth, mingling previously isolated cultures, changing political perceptions and creating new economic zones and alliances.

There is a recognisable cycle in the history of the development of aviation: a phase of pioneering and innovation followed first by a military application, then by commercial exploitation.

The pioneering era of near-Earth space flight is really over. The early military application – observation – has been going on for some time; 'Star Wars' is nearly upon us. The commercialisation of space is under way: information speeds round the Earth via satellites, businessmen can have electronic conferences rather than travel to meet each other, the Earth's resources are being sought out and mapped, pharmaceuticals and other high-value materials are being developed in zero gravity and will soon be manufactured in space. The Americans are planning a space station for permanent habitation and further exploration of the Moon and the planets will follow. Just as surely as settlers followed Christopher Columbus from Europe to America, so a new generation of techno-settlers will colonise space.

People are the impetus behind progress and the impetus behind the rapid advance in aviation has been pilots, the relatively small number of pilots who push back the frontiers of aviation, who push aircraft to the limits and beyond, finding out, in the air, how to control them, how to build better aircraft, how to make them fly faster, further, higher, how to control bigger and bigger machines, and who find new military and commercial applications for them.

The pilots in this book have been chosen because of their contribution to the progress of aviation. Whether they are well known like Blériot, Lindbergh and Richthofen, or more obscure like Cody and McCudden, none of them has been chosen because they have unique qualities; there are other stories which illustrate many of the same points and there has usually been a queue of other pilots striving to achieve the things they did. Usually they became well known in public or inside aviation circles precisely because they not only did what they did, but because they did it by beating somebody else to it.

Competitiveness, in peace and war, has been a major ingredient in the rapid progress of aviation. There is competitiveness between individual pilots and competitiveness between nations, especially in research and development flying. Doing something new with an aeroplane is a challenge which cannot be resisted and it is being first which counts. Nobody wants to be second-best, nobody wants to be second to do something: who remembers the second pilot to fly the Channel, the second pilot to fly the Atlantic, the second pilot to fly faster than sound? In the case of the fighter pilot, being second-best is usually literally fatal. Flying to the limits is a pilot's way of expressing himself, of showing his full potential: like an athlete, a politician or any competitive endeavour, proving that one is the best or being first is vital.

Because what they do is so far beyond the experience of all but a few people, there has always been a popular fascination with pilots at the forefront of development flying; an aura of excellence shines from them, they are ascribed superhuman qualities, they become superheroes. But most tend to shy away from publicity, or appear to: the Wright Brothers genuinely hated it, Blériot loved it and capitalised on it, Lindbergh wanted to control it, Chuck Yeager can take it or leave it and John Young is curiously reminiscent of the Wrights.

Man does progress through technology: wood and fabric, rivets and bonding compounds, composite materials and aluminium alloys, wingspans, engines, horsepowers and thickness/cord ratios are vital but they don't do anything without people; the story of aviation is, like all the best stories, a story of people, a story of pilots.

Index